MONEY TALKS

ELLIE
AUSTIN -WILLIAMS

MONEY
TALKS

A LIFESTYLE GUIDE
FOR FINANCIAL
WELLBEING

WATKINS
1893

Money Talks
Ellie Austin-Williams

First published in the UK and USA in 2024 by
Watkins, an imprint of Watkins Media Limited
Unit 11, Shepperton House, 83–93 Shepperton Road
London N1 3DF

enquiries@watkinspublishing.com

Commissioning Editor: Lucy Carroll
Project Editor: Brittany Willis
Copyeditor: Sue Lascelles
Head of Design: Karen Smith
Designer: Steve Williamson
Production: Uzma Taj

A CIP record for this book is available from the British Library

ISBN: 978-1-78678-799-6 (Paperback)
ISBN: 978-1-78678-798-9 (eBook)

10 9 8 7 6 5 4 3 2 1

Printed in the United Kingdom by TJ Books Limited

www.watkinspublishing.com

MIX
Paper from
responsible sources
FSC® C013056

To the women who raised me to believe
that I can make my dreams a reality

CONTENTS

INTRODUCTION

IT'S (NOT) ABOUT THE MONEY

This isn't your stereotypical book about money. There are plenty of books out there that will walk you through the ABCs of money management, from what type of bank accounts you need through to understanding how credit cards work, or how to make it onto that first rung of the property ladder. But the thing about money is that for all that society tries to simplify it and boil it down to tips and tricks, practical wisdom and sensible habits, it remains a highly emotional subject. The emotions tied to money are powerful – from fear to security, embarrassment to opportunity – and for most people, they are deeply rooted in our brains. Yet whether we like it or not, money plays a part in everyday life for all of us, whatever our circumstances, financial knowledge or our means. And it's notable that for even the most logical person in the world, decisions about money can prove to be a stumbling block that appears out of nowhere, blindsiding even the most rational of minds.

And yet the majority of the world continues to operate by a set of money rules which imply that if you play the game correctly, you'll come out on top. *Work hard and earn money. Work harder, earn more. Save your income and receive financial security. Invest now and become wealthy later. Spend less and get richer.* Turns out, it's not quite as simple as it sounds and I'm about to tell you why. Money isn't just about the numbers, but so much more.

WHY MONEY TALKS

My journey into the financial wellbeing space began long before I started speaking about the topic openly. My earliest recollection of engaging with finance came during my teenage years, when my grandfather gave me a hefty *Financial Times* book on investing. I'd always known he had a keen interest in stocks and shares, so I took an interest in the topic too. However, when I saw the dense pages of this introduction to the financial market, the book quickly found a safe spot in the back of a drawer. There my interest in finance remained until years later, at the start of my career in my early 20s. After an extended period as a student, when I first started to earn a regular salary I quickly realized that I had absolutely no clue how to make wise financial decisions, both for the short and long term. As a 20-something living in London, I wanted to enjoy my new monthly bank balance and experience the world, yet I equally knew I had ambitions to secure myself financially in the future. I'd always dreamed of travelling, having my own home and being able to treat my family, who supported me through my school years.

Naturally, I started to look for resources to help answer some of the many questions I had about financial literacy. I scoured the internet and bookshops, only to find myself stuck at a dead end with two polarizing camps trying to lure me in. At one extreme, there was plenty of literature set on the idea that I needed to stop spending money and start saving every spare penny immediately if I ever wanted to reach a state of financial security. In this camp, all forms of debt are considered bad, spending more than necessary on essentials such as housing is seen as wasteful, and the aim is simply to save as much of your income as possible. For a girl like me, who enjoyed travel and was living in bustling southwest London at the time, this didn't strike a chord. At the other end of the spectrum, the core advice was you only live once; why spend your younger years saving money when you can spend it all? According to this viewpoint, there's a time to make sensible choices but that's for later, not now, so stop being boring and spend the money.

Although I may have been quick to jump at the opportunity to book a weekend away with the girls, I still had bigger-picture financial aspirations. Surely, I thought, these aren't the only options out there? There has to be a better option, or a middle ground. A way to make wise, informed decisions for the future while still allowing myself to have fun in the present and enjoy myself. After all, life isn't just about accumulating as much as possible, yet when money is such an integral part of how the world works there must be a way to feel in control and good about it. I figured that if I was looking for this information and knowledge, surely there were plenty of others out there in the same boat.

Fast forward several years, a career change and accompanying lifestyle pivot later – along with countless hours of reading, learning and knowledge building – and I find myself writing this book. From taking the step into the personal finance field and becoming a commissioned financial writer in major publications, to training as a certified financial coach in order to better understand money behaviours, I have dedicated the last five years to understanding what really matters when it comes to money – from what makes people take the financial decisions they do (clue: it isn't logic), through to the narratives we tell ourselves subconsciously about money, wealth and privilege. Through building an online platform, I've been in the fortunate position to speak to hundreds of individuals about their thoughts, opinions, hopes and fears about money that they haven't even shared with their inner circle.

Yet there's only so much depth in which you can explore a topic in an Instagram post or TikTok video. It soon became clear to me that our lives are scattered with moments, relationships and interactions where money fundamentally impacts our experience. From the friendships we form on the first day at school, to the wedding invitations we receive as adults, the role of money is everywhere – and still no one dares to acknowledge it. Until now. Throughout this book, I explore the most influential parts of our lives where, whether we're aware of it or not, money plays a part. Combining statistics and data with first-hand experiences and expert commentary, *Money Talks* unpacks the complicated, often confusing way that money shapes our lives and provides actionable insights to deal with the challenges that issues around money and wealth can throw our way.

THE FEMALE FINANCIAL EMERGENCY

Looking over the history of the financial sector, it's clear to see that the world of banking and finance has been built by, and for, men. By no means does this mean that men don't have financial challenges or struggles too; however, countless years of data and research have shown that by almost every measure of financial security or confidence, men fare better than their female counterparts. History has a major part to play in this: only 50 years ago, women across the world had significantly fewer financial rights than men. It wasn't until 1974 that American women could apply for credit without a male signatory, or 1982 in the UK when women were allowed to spend their money in a pub without being refused service.[1]

But despite the passing of time and progress being made in many respects, the needle is shifting at an extremely slow pace when it comes to closing gender gaps across the financial board. Women continue to fall behind men in terms of pay, investments, wealth and pensions, leaving them less financially secure and experiencing lower levels of financial wellbeing. The Money and Pensions Service put it bluntly: "There is a financial emergency for women. Women's financial wellbeing outcomes, amplified by low confidence and low engagement with advice and guidance, are significantly worse than men's."

It's time that we change the story.

THE SEARCH FOR FINANCIAL WELLBEING

It's safe to say that the last few years have thrown a curveball into the lives of almost every person on the planet, with a pandemic causing chaos to global economies and a war triggering worldwide inflation. With consecutive shocks to the financial situations of households of all shapes, sizes and incomes, the concept of financial wellbeing has risen in the consciousness of both individuals and businesses. But what actually *is* financial wellbeing? To best understand how our finances fit into our wider wellbeing, let's take a holistic view of wellbeing first. There are typically thought to be four pillars of wellness – physical, mental, social and financial – which combine together to provide a foundation or platform for overall human wellbeing and happiness.

THE FOUR PILLARS OF WELLNESS

Focusing on one or two of these pillars can lead to improvement in specific areas, but only when you look after all four pillars can you reach optimum wellbeing. Wellbeing isn't an end destination, either; it's an ongoing journey full of highs and lows, wins and challenges, and financial wellbeing is no different.

Of the four pillars of wellness, mainstream society tends to put the most emphasis on promoting physical wellbeing. From a young age, we're encouraged to pay attention to our physical wellbeing through movement and nutrition. Increasingly over the last ten years or so, there has been a notable rise in discourse surrounding mental wellbeing too, both in terms of how critical it is to pay attention to our own mental health, alongside the importance of supporting the mental wellbeing of those around us. Closely tied to mental wellbeing is social wellbeing, as connection to others and community play a key part in maintaining our mental wellbeing. Loneliness and social disconnection contribute to poorer mental health, whereas strong social networks can help support you in navigating tricky times in your life. And financial wellbeing? It's the pillar of wellbeing that for so long has remained in the shadows, yet arguably has the biggest impact on our lives.

With over a quarter of adults feeling stressed about money every day, financial wellbeing has a knock-on effect on the mental wellbeing of millions of adults, causing more worry than work, health and family matters do.[2] The picture is crystal clear that we're heading for a financial wellbeing crisis, yet for too long the approach to financial wellbeing has centred on budgeting tips and savings hacks, rather than digging deeper into the root of the issue. After all, if we could budget our way out of poverty then we'd surely be living in a completely different world? The truth is that money isn't just practical, but emotional and political too. Diving head first into the conversation about financial wellbeing requires us to take off our blinkers, set aside our assumptions or biases and look at the way that both we as individuals and the society we live in address the topics of money, wealth and privilege. Only when we look at our everyday interactions, our gut feelings and our deep-rooted beliefs about money can we start to understand what financial wellbeing truly means for each one of us and how we can get closer to improving our own unique relationship with money.

LET'S TALK ABOUT PRIVILEGE

There's one issue that comes hand in hand with the conversations throughout the course of this book that it'd be careless to skip over, and that's financial privilege. Privilege manifests itself in many different forms, and when it comes to money then the way privilege impacts our experiences, opportunities and challenges can be vast. Although many other aspects of privilege come into play when we talk about money, such as gender and race, the economic privilege underpinning many of the discussions throughout this book refers to a level of financial stability or wealth that gives you access to opportunities or advantages that others may not have. In the so-called race of life, financial privilege can serve as a ten-second head start for hitting other financial goals, such as funding education, landing a sought-after job role or getting on the housing ladder.

Although the role of privilege means that equality of opportunity is sometimes a distant dream, by acknowledging our own economic privilege we can be more aware of the ways in which we have benefited from our circumstances and act to try to level the playing field. Privilege is too often considered to be a dirty word, and many conversations about privilege descend into a defence of how much effort or hard work people have put into achieving their goals, without the acknowledgement of how privilege can help provide a platform for us to flourish. While it's true that financial privilege alone is no guarantee of happiness or success, there are plenty of studies which show that the combination of economic privilege and effort can lead to outcomes that those without an equal level of privilege may struggle to achieve, despite their hardest efforts. So, as you turn the pages of this book, I would encourage you to explore the way that financial privilege can impact all facets of our lives – from work to relationships to motherhood – and to start to reflect on your own journey with money, taking note of the role that financial privilege has played in your life. Only once we have an awareness of the cards we've been dealt that have influenced where we are today can we start to advocate and lift up other women and push for greater female financial wellbeing in our own circles, communities and afar.

FINDING YOUR RICH LIFE

At the root of taking steps toward improving your financial wellbeing, there is one question that I believe underpins everything else: what do you want your life to look like, truly? It's a question that frequently evades us, as we get swept along in the checklist of adulthood and milestones that society expects us to meet. Even when we step away from the well-trodden path, there are often ideas embedded in our brains from a young age about what our life *should* look like. Yet only when we really tune in to ourselves and understand what makes us tick, what matters to us and what motivates us, can we start to piece together a picture of our own "rich" life. The term "rich" tends to evoke an image dripping in gold or luxury in a *Succession*-like style, yet the word itself has layers of deeper meaning. *Collins Dictionary* defines a rich life as "one that is interesting because it is full of different events and activities", with no mention whatsoever of wealth or material resources. So here I challenge you to take some time out, switch your phone onto aeroplane mode and ask yourself: what does my rich life look like?

Financial wellbeing is intrinsically linked to our idea of a rich life, as one of the core jigsaw pieces in the financial wellbeing puzzle involves separating our own value from our bank balance. The exercises in this book are designed to help you understand what wealth truly means to you, because when you have a clear idea of what your own rich life looks like, you'll have a north star to guide you when it comes to making difficult decisions relating to your work, money and lifestyle. Without clarity on your values as an individual, it can become all too easy to find yourself sacrificing your financial – and mental – wellbeing in pursuit of riches. Understanding your own "why" is not easy, though; much like the lack of practical financial education at school, there's a gaping hole in the education system around helping individuals really connect to their passions and purpose. As we'll explore throughout this book, increasingly this lack of support early on will manifest itself later in life, with more and more adults today seeking meaning and fulfilment in their life and in work.

Wherever you are in your journey toward building better financial wellbeing, I hope that in reading this book you'll be inspired to dig deeper into your own relationship with money. Because taking steps toward improving your financial wellbeing can open the door to a life full of purpose that brings you joy and lights you up . . .

LIVE TO WORK, OR WORK TO LIVE?

①

Let's start out with some perspective. The average person spends one-third of their entire life at work. Yes, one-third. That comes in at around 85,000 hours, more or less.[1] That's a whole lot of time that we spend working, so it's only natural that increasing numbers of people are looking for work that brings more to their everyday life than simply paying the bills. But the trouble is that the modern world of work is complicated, to say the least. When you do work that you enjoy, you can find a sense of fulfilment that lights you up; yet find yourself in a bad work environment and you could end up facing huge amounts of stress and anxiety. And that's all before we even mention the "M" word.

So why is it that our relationship with work isn't straight-forward these days? From a young age at school, we're told that if we work hard then success will come. It's a simple message instilled in us during our formative years, so it's no surprise that we take it to be true in the workplace as well. Add on top a slice of popular culture messaging (remember when UK influencer Molly-Mae told us we all have the same 24 hours in a day as Beyoncé?), along with the "work hard and you'll succeed" narrative often promoted by our elders and no wonder we're a generation working harder than ever but struggling to see the financial rewards we were promised. Turns out, in the modern world of work there's no sure-fire guarantee that hard work pays off in a monetary sense. The disconnect between the messages so many of us grew up believing to be true and the reality we face has led to confusion among many 20- and 30-somethings about what we're really working for. In the absence of the material or lifestyle benefits we hoped for, ever more people are turning away from working themselves into the ground and "bare minimum Mondays" are on the rise. There's never been a trickier time to navigate the world of work.

So if hard work alone isn't the answer to success, how do you build a successful career? What does success even look like today, in a tough economic environment that seems so different to the world faced by generations before us? Is purpose in your career more important than a pay package and if so, how can we pivot our career to find something that fills our cup? And that's before we add the role of gender in the workplace into the mix. While women in the workplace are much more visible and taking more senior positions than 50 years ago, it's a hard-fought battle and the challenges that the modern world of work presents for women are far from over. Today, the reality of the workplace for women still has many of us asking: can women really have it all and, actually, do we want it all?

THE PATH TO THE PROMISED LAND

As a cookie-cutter millennial, my career to date is the epitome of squiggly. The path to where I am right now starts way back in school, where I decided that I wanted to be successful. What does success mean to an 11-year-old? I now wonder. Looking back, it's clear that my picture of success back then revolved around shiny things, and from a young age I set off in the pursuit of riches. Sitting here now over 20 years later, I wonder what on earth the younger me would think about the career trajectory that led me to where I am right now. About the fact that I veered off the path I'd worked single-mindedly to get myself onto for over half a decade, with its potential to fast track me to a hefty bank balance (along with a whole lot of stress and burnout), in pursuit of something . . . completely different. Let's take a quick trip down memory lane.

My decision to become a lawyer wasn't a long-standing childhood dream. In fact, my first career plan was to be an air hostess and fly around the world to exotic destinations, before I realized I was more interested in actually being the passenger rather than serving them. Becoming a lawyer was a decision I made as I sat in my university halls during the first year of my Modern Languages degree. A few months into my first year at college, I decided that I needed to figure out what I wanted to do as a job when I graduated, so I headed to the careers office and picked up a copy of *The Times Top 100 Graduate Employers*. In the absence of any meaningful career's guidance available – either at school or at university – at 18 years old I concluded that the answer must be enclosed in those pages. For anyone who hasn't come across the guide before, it's not an overstatement to describe it as an A to Z of corporate careers, with a sprinkling of public sector roles on top. As I flicked through the pages, past consulting giants and accountancy firms, dismissing them as too mathematical, I stopped at the profile of a major city law firm. I looked at the job description, required characteristics and particularly the starting salary of £39,000 (approx. $48,500) – and decided that I would be a lawyer. And that's how it started.

Before I go any further, I want to acknowledge that my journey into a legal career was by no means the experience a lot of people have. Landing a training contract isn't easy; thousands of young people aspire to be lawyers, spending huge amounts to fund their studies and struggling for years to get a foot in the door. I worked hard at school and university, don't get me wrong; but I also learned how to jump through the hoops required to get in the door early on. Plus, alongside the part I played in getting the job, financial and class privilege came into play. I attended well-regarded schools where I had achieved above-average grades. I went on to higher education, and I had an English-teacher parent to help proofread all my application letters. From the moment I decided I wanted to be a lawyer, I had laser-focus; it influenced every decision I made at university, from where I spent my year abroad to the dissertation I wrote. I knew that becoming a lawyer was my ticket to the salary I wanted to earn, but I hadn't once stopped to consider whether the job – or the lifestyle that comes with it – matched up to my idealistic idea of success.

There are an endless number of reasons why so many millennials have found themselves in professional services jobs, corporate careers or white-collar jobs. Specific job titles were sold to many of us as the route to a fulfilling and financially comfortable life, only to find that the reality doesn't look anything like the picture-postcard lifestyle we'd imagined. For many 1980s and 1990s kids, choosing a career wasn't about following your passion or embracing your creative spark. School career services prioritized making a practical decision to set yourself up for the future financially, rather than filling your cup with work that lights you up each day. The influence of our caregivers was significant too; for some, following in the footsteps of parents with comfortable middle-class lifestyles seemed an inevitable route, while for others, their working-class parents promoted white-collar careers as the answer to the financial security they didn't have themselves. But in the absence of helpful guidance and relevant reference points, along with a dramatically different economic landscape, it's no wonder many of us have found ourselves questioning the career paths we pursued.

Having spoken to a range of women about their own experiences, I have found that the falsehoods planted in their minds from a young age about work, careers and success span far and wide. From the idea that only an office job qualifies as a proper job, through to the belief that careers in hospitality weren't long-term rewarding job options, it's stark to see how heavily influenced we are by those around us when it comes to our choices about work. At the start of her career working in luxury clothing retail, Caitlin, a store manager, found herself constantly questioned by customers and her family about her choice of employment: "Family members ask, 'Are you still working retail? Do you have plans for the future?' and then they're all shocked and confused when I say no – this is my career." Now don't get me wrong, I don't think that older generations purposefully sent us down the wrong path and intentionally misled us about careers, success and contentment, but many of them did take it for granted that the well-trodden path that served them well in the 1980s and 1990s would produce the same results, not factoring in that the world in which millennials became adults in would be fundamentally different. The formula that worked so well 20 years ago no longer leads to the same results as it once did, and it's only now that lots of us are realizing that we've not only been dealt a different hand, but that we're playing a totally different game.

WHO AND WHAT HAS INFLUENCED YOUR CAREER CHOICES?

Before we dive into what that world looks like today, take a moment to ask yourself:

- What led you to the career and work life you find yourself in today?

- How did your parents, caregivers and educators influence your decisions and shape your choices?

Taking a moment to reflect on your own journey can help you to better understand how you feel about your current work life and identify any desires you may still have for your career.

TO INTERN, OR NOT TO INTERN?

The world of work is closely tied to our sense of identity and provokes a whole host of questions about our choices and values, yet the path to our first job often requires stepping stones which can take the form of work experience or, in some sectors, an elusive internship. On paper, the idea of an internship is simple and effective. The aim of an internship is to provide a student with the opportunity to have a practical, hands-on experience of working in a field they hope to pursue long term, along with a chance to make connections and a good impression on potential employers. Yet the reality can look vastly different; in certain industries, unpaid, competitive internships mean that places are reserved solely for those with high-powered connections and the funds to finance weeks of unpaid labour.

Before you even get a foot in the door of certain sectors – such as publishing and fashion – you can find yourself struggling to access the traditional career path simply because of not being middle class and wealthy. In 2013, Melissa landed herself a role at a fashion company in London with a pay packet of £25 per week, for ten months. To make ends meet and pursue her job, Melissa lodged with a family and worked as a nanny in her spare time in exchange for cheap rent. Despite enjoying the worlds of fashion and design, Melissa realized that working in the design industry would make her financial goals significantly harder to achieve and so eventually moved to the financial services industry to secure a more stable financial future. Melissa isn't alone, either. Despite the increasing spotlight on social mobility issues caused by unpaid or poorly paid internships, there is still a long way to go when it comes to levelling the playing field for job opportunities across the board. For lots of people, pursuing a career in a field they felt drawn to simply wasn't viable financially, while for others the more traditionally stable, better paid paths were encouraged from early on. It's clear that even before we start to earn, our unique financial circumstances influence our approaches toward choosing a career and the key factors taken into account when choosing a route to pursue.

MIND THE GENDER GAP

When I entered the workforce in the 2000s, I believed that being female in the workplace would have little to no impact on my career. For many young women like me, the progress made by our predecessors in breaking barriers and paving the way for women to rise up the ranks of careers once dominated by men inspired hope and excitement about the world of work. Yet behind the scenes, the fight for gender equality at work is still far from over. The gender pay gap still persists across the globe, despite initiatives to encourage companies to monitor pay and address inequalities in compensation – including base salaries and bonuses – that impact women simply as a result of their gender. According to the Global Gender Gap Report 2020, at the rate of progress at the time of publication then it was projected to take another 100 years to achieve gender equality.[2] And that was before the pandemic, which saw women disproportionately affected, with as many as two million women forced to consider taking a step backward in their career or leaving the workforce to care for young children.[3]

Female representation at senior levels still remains a challenge too, even in industries where graduate recruitment consistently achieves an even gender split. Particularly in high-pressure, demanding industries, structural issues and work culture at many organizations have left high-performing, ambitious women with little choice but to leave senior positions if they wish to have a family. Talented women with a desire to work hard and reach their career potential are being sidelined because they simply don't fit the traditional model of how management – often led by males – believe the company should run. So although times have changed significantly for women in work compared to those experienced by our grandparents and predecessors, we have a long way to go to close the gap and change the narrative for females that follow in our own footsteps.

HOW TO PROMOTE GENDER EQUALITY AT WORK

Whether you're new to your workplace or you've been at a company for years, promoting gender equality is a positive action you can take to influence and encourage progress. There are three key steps that organizations can take to improve the situation for female employees and thereby retain talented employees:

Increase salary transparency

One contributing factor to the gender pay gap is a lack of salary transparency, enabling companies to pay males more for the same work carried out as a female co-worker. Pushing for more salary transparency can help reduce the likelihood of such gaps persisting.

Create flexible policies

The rise of remote working has opened the door for many men and women to work in a way that helps them manage both family and work responsibilities. Through supporting flexible work and encouraging employees to make the most of parental leave policies, companies can retain talent and push women forward in their careers.

Educate teams on gender bias

Although consciously organizations and leaders may support gender equality, unconscious gender bias has a significant impact on hiring and promotion decisions and can work against women looking to progress their careers. Putting in place processes during recruitment to identify bias and reduce unconscious bias can increase opportunities offered to women in the workplace.

THE RISE AND FALL OF THE GIRLBOSS

Growing up in the 2000s, from a young age I looked up to women in high places and aspired to emulate the icons that I could see. My ambitions started out looking up to superstars such as Britney Spears and Christina Aguilera, but I soon realized that my lack of musical talent was a pretty huge hurdle to pop stardom. My own talents aside, watching the careers of famous women reach stratospheric levels during my formative years and charting their rise became a source of inspiration to work harder and believe that I could do anything I set my mind to.

During my teenage years, the idea of working for myself had never entered my mind, but when I look back I can see that even before we hit peak hustle era, I imagined being a powerful, high-flying business woman. Watching *Legally Blonde*, I saw Elle Woods take on the legal world in high heels, followed a few years later by *Suits* where Jessica Pearson ran the firm. It might not have looked like the picture of being a girlboss we've since come to know, but it's clear that for many of us from a young age, the main narrative about how to win in your career as an ambitious woman revolved around leaning in and stepping up to the challenge of succeeding in a male-centred work environment.

The term "girlboss" first became popularized in 2014 when Sophia Amoruso, founder of the American retailer Nasty Gal, used the term to title her autobiography about her ambition and success in a male-dominated world. At first glance, the message behind the title and the concept of a girlboss seemed clear: to inspire a generation of young women to become leaders and empower them. Yet over the years that #girlboss dominated social media posts, powder pink notebooks and T-shirts galore, it became increasingly evident that there's a darker undertone to the girlboss message.

What is the difference between a girlboss and a regular boss? The uncomfortable truth is that when you pause to think about it, many people still picture a boss as a male figure. The use of the gender qualifier "girl" in girlboss draws attention to the gender aspect, infantilizing the female in question and reinforcing the idea that women are not naturally bosses. Men are still widely considered to be instinctive leaders, in contrast to women. As the creative global platform Refinery29 put it, rather than sending a strong, meaningful message to young women, girlboss culture in fact became "a marketable form of feminism . . . which sells hollow empowerment instead of high-lighting the less palatable facts of life for working women".[4]

HUSTLE CULTURE

It's almost impossible to talk about girlboss culture without looking at the rise of hustle culture over recent years. More than ever, it's become near normalized to juggle a full-time job with a side hustle to earn more income, highlighting the fact that for many, one source of income is no longer enough to live comfortably in the modern world. The economic fallout of the 2008 financial crash meant that millions of millennials faced a fragile, unstable job market as they entered the world of work and quickly found themselves working 40-hour weeks, only to end the month in the red. In times of economic instability, companies are quick to respond and one major reaction is to cut costs.

Inevitably, the more junior employees in an organization often contribute the least financially to a company as they are yet to build a client base or gain years of experience, so they find themselves most disposable to corporations looking to boost their bottom line. In 2009, as a response to the global recession, graduate job vacancies in the UK fell by 8.9 per cent and two-thirds of employers implemented a recruitment freeze.[5] Similarly in the US, the situation has been bleak for graduates, according to a report in the *New York Times*.[6] Typically, it takes five to ten years to recover from the impact of a recession, leaving those entering the workforce exposed to a hostile environment with limited opportunities and low wage growth at the start of their careers. Coupled with historic house price inflation that has seen property prices rise to stratospheric levels, the realization that even an above-average salary and hard work will leave you short of a few hundred thousand for a roof over your head hit home for many, paving the way for hustle culture to boom. And while there's nothing problematic about tapping into your skills to build a business or making some extra money in your spare time, there's a sinister side to hustle culture too.

Hustle culture glamorizes overworking as aspirational, attributing the success of entrepreneurs and business women to their relentless work schedule and, frankly, their lack of sleep.

At the same time as pinning up burnout as a badge of honour, hustle culture often ignores the many other contributing factors to a success story that we might not know about from the outside looking in. I'm talking about the partner that pays the bills, the nest egg to fall back on, or even the stomach-churning risk-taking that, nine times out of ten, doesn't pay off. And gone are the days where a hobby or side project was only something you did for fun; in the 21st century, every aspect of your life can be commoditized and turned into a money-making machine.

But not everyone agrees that hustle culture is toxic. There's a strong case that the ability to turn the skills you already have into making money in your spare time has had a bigger positive impact on women than men, especially during the pandemic lockdown in 2020. Thousands of women outside of employment, often as a result of the need to be flexible around childcare, have been able to start earning an income through setting up a side hustle such as freelancing online or private tutoring that works around their other responsibilities, in some cases starting hugely successful companies that allow them to leave their previous work behind.

Chloe Carmichael was a serial side hustler who tried many things to make extra money before deciding to set up Chloe's Deal Club, with no intention of running it as a business. She explains: "I started it purely as a hobby and never intended it to be my job. I started it because I genuinely enjoy it and love helping people save money." But building a side hustle and working full-time isn't always as easy as it looks online, and Chloe is keen to make it clear that starting a demanding side hustle alongside working full-time isn't for the faint-hearted: "I'm not going to lie, [working full-time and running a side hustle] was challenging and I was burnt out. I was constantly glued to my phone between working full-time as a social media manager and running my own social media accounts. My screen time was a minimum of ten hours a day and I spent most of my free time working on my side hustle, so I knew something had to give, which is when I finally resigned from my full-time job."

Perhaps, then, in a world where we can lean in and hustle hard or choose to tune out the noise and build our career quietly, the answer is that there isn't anything inherently right or wrong with a side hustle. Since the dawn of time, there have been people who thrive under pressure and hard work, coexisting with those who seek a calm, quiet work life with no stress. So perhaps now is the time to ask yourself: what is your own appetite for work? How much do you crave a balance between work and your life outside of your career? What does a good work life mean to you?

ARE WE REDEFINING AMBITION?

It isn't that long ago that the career path you set down in your late teens or early 20s was likely to be your career for life. Work facilitated the rest of your life, and often loyalty to an employer paid off with generous work benefits and a feeling of camaraderie. Yet the impact of the financial crisis and a shift in the global economic landscape has meant that over the last few decades the deal between employers and employees that kept so many people in one career or company for long periods of time has disintegrated.

When the expectation that you work hard, earn a fair wage and climb a steady career ladder was a reality, swallowing the pill of doing a job you don't love wasn't too hard. But gone are the days where loyalty pays off and working tirelessly in many sectors no longer guarantees a comfortable standard of living. With wage stagnation, creeping work hours and increasing expectations, the trade-off that is required between work and play has skewed beyond recognition. Without the deal on the table that previous generations had on offer, it isn't a surprise that a London School of Business and Finance study found that two-thirds (66 per cent) of workers aged between 18 and 34 want to change careers and increasingly people are doing so.[7]

Alice Stapleton is a career change coach for those in their 20s and 30s, helping people who feel lost in their current careers to find a new direction. When I asked Alice why career change is becoming so much more common among millennials and Gen Z, compared to older generations, she told me, "The Pandemic in 2020 forced a lot of Millennials to re-evaluate their careers. With the 'luxuries' of work stripped away, many finally had the time, brain space, and money to face the niggles they'd been putting off for years. It's hard to avoid what you really do for a living when it's just you and your laptop at home for two years!"

It's commonly said nowadays that another factor at play is the desire for purpose at work among younger generations, but is this in fact a falsehood that isn't reflected in the decisions people make about their careers? Alice says, "I think that Millennials and Gen Z are becoming more and more aware of the impact they want their lives to have. They want to feel like they matter, that their work has a positive impact, and that they spend their days doing something that carries meaning and feels worthwhile to them. Yet many fall into jobs they don't particularly like after education, just because they want to start earning money, so they take the first thing they're offered. So, in order to start ticking these boxes, a career change is often required."

From both Alice's expertise and my own experience of speaking to countless 20- and 30-somethings, it seems clear that increasingly people are seeking more from their careers outside of a paycheque each month. But there's still one question that comes to mind whenever I speak to people about the prospect of work being fulfilling and financially beneficial. Is work the right place to search for fulfilment and pursue our passions, or do we need to reset our expectations? Is it realistic to aspire to a career that provides passion and that pays well – or should we settle for one of the two? And what if work is simply just a way to facilitate other life ambitions – isn't that a win in itself?

ALIGNING PURPOSE WITH PAYCHEQUES

Annie is a lawyer in her early 30s living in London. After spending the early years of her career in corporate law in Melbourne, Annie moved to London to work for one of the most prestigious law firms in the city. I asked Annie about what attracted her to the corporate law and whether she enjoyed working there. She replied, "I liked most of the job because I like being challenged and I like working with nice people. That's probably the best way to put it. I like working with nice people, smart people, and so all of that was there. What I didn't enjoy was when I felt like I was being asked to make sacrifices that I didn't think were worthwhile."

Having worked at one of the biggest law firms in the country, Annie decided that it was time to make a change and move away from a six-figure corporate salary to work for an NGO as an in-house counsel. I wanted to know whether it occurred to Annie to stay put in the corporate world because the money was worth the demands of the job. She told me, "At the time I was at the end, I could not keep doing a job that I cared so little about, and that stole so much time from me. So the difference in pay had stopped being worth it to me. I was like, I know that I've been given this money to miss events with friends, to not be able to rock up things, to not sleep, to be stressed. I'm being paid for that – and it's not worth it anymore."

Annie isn't alone, either. A workplace study by PwC found that work–life balance is important to 95 per cent of millennials; more so than financial reward, with flexible working hours being a higher priority than cash bonuses. This doesn't mean that earning a good salary isn't important – it goes without saying that for the most part, people are looking for fair compensation for their work. Yet it seems that simply throwing money at employees to purchase their free time and social lives might not be cutting it any longer; people are looking for meaningful work that ticks more boxes than a paycheque.

The concept of meaningful work isn't one-size-fits-all. However, figuring out what meaningful work looks like for each individual entails reflecting on some key questions about what we each consider to be meaningful or meaningless. Meaningful work isn't reserved for those working in the charity sector or healthcare; meaning can come from alignment with your interests, feeling that the work you do has a greater purpose than a bottom line or in fact how a job facilitates meaning in other areas of your life.

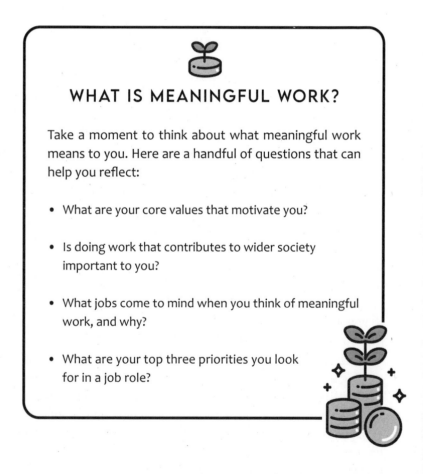

WHAT IS MEANINGFUL WORK?

Take a moment to think about what meaningful work means to you. Here are a handful of questions that can help you reflect:

- What are your core values that motivate you?

- Is doing work that contributes to wider society important to you?

- What jobs come to mind when you think of meaningful work, and why?

- What are your top three priorities you look for in a job role?

FINDING YOUR NEW FIELD

You've decided your career isn't working for you, but what comes next? The idea of changing careers can be exciting, yet even when you know your current career isn't the one, more often than not there's a gaping hole when it comes to the question of what to do instead. Unless you're one of the lucky people who has a clear-cut alternative career plan in the back of their mind waiting on ice, figuring out how to make a living in a completely different direction to your existing path can keep you stuck where you are for years. Working out how to take the first step forward might just be the most challenging part, but it's also the most important.

Anyone that has come to a career crossroads has probably tried out trawling job boards online, looking for a spark of inspiration or excitement, but career change coach Alice explains why often this is a fruitless exercise when you're looking for a meaningful career change or a new direction: "For too long, we've relied on internet job boards to find a new career. But you can only apply for what you can see. Think of it like a fish bowl – if you're a tiny fish just swimming around in the same old pond all day, you'll only ever come across the same ideas and options within that pond. But what if you were to jump out of that pond and swim around in a completely different one?"

You might be thinking, "That makes a whole lot of sense – but how do I find another pond to swim around in?" It's one of the most common questions that comes up for aspiring career changers, who Alice works with on a daily basis. She says, "Clients often tell me that they don't know where to start with their career change, because they don't have any passions or interests. But how true is this really? I often wonder whether we sometimes believe we don't have any passions, because, as a society, what being 'passionate' looks like these days has been skewed. Yet if we're open and flexible to what this 'passion' looks like, and how long it may last, it's easier to find it in a career."

So, if you're thinking about a career change then why not take the pressure off finding the perfect option and allow yourself to think creatively outside the box? If you're unhappy or stuck, stop telling yourself that the right time will come and think about how you can start to move forward. But is there a right time to make a big career change? Alice doesn't believe so. "I don't think there is ever a 'right' time," she says. "The clients I work with have one thing in common, though – they're ready to move forward because they know they don't want to be stuck doing what they're currently doing anymore. As long as the initial commitment and motivation is there, the rest can be worked out one small step at a time."

THE CAREER SUNK-COST FALLACY

Even if you realize that your current career path isn't for the long term, it's not always as easy as 1, 2, 3 to pivot direction and change careers. Especially if you're someone who has committed years of your life to pursuing qualifications – not to mention signed up to thousands of pounds in student loans – changing career direction can be daunting. To understand how to deal with this challenge, I spoke to Bari, a dietician turned head of marketing, about how she found her career change after spending so much time building her credentials as a dietician.

She told me, "I had a huge identity crisis, first of all, because I racked up over $100,000 of student debt to be a dietician with a master's degree from UCL in this really niche field. So I thought, well why did I do that? What's the point of doing all that if I'm not going to even pursue it? It was really scary. I toyed with it for months. Do I make the leap? Do I not make the leap? Do I have to have one foot in the door of nutrition or not?"

After investing so much time and money in her first career, does Bari ever regret the decision to make the career change and put the dietician work behind her? The answer is a resounding no. "I don't ever regret it," she explains. "I feel like the career change that I've had has led me to so much like personal growth and career growth. For my personality, I realize that this is a much better fit for my natural skills and how I like to work and progress. You don't know when you're 18. And I left this situation feeling nutrition is a passion and a hobby. It's not my career."

Whether you find yourself nodding along and can relate to Bari's experience, or you're early on in exploring your options, the natural next step is to ask yourself what your "better fit" career might look like. I asked Bari for any words of wisdom for anyone seeking to find their better fit and how to begin the discovery process. Bari summarized the process in three core questions.

WHAT SHAPE COULD YOUR "BETTER FIT" CAREER TAKE?

Using Bari's example as inspiration, here are some questions to ask yourself to get the ball rolling if you are thinking about changing career. Take a moment to reflect on them and write down your answers.

- **What are your values?** What are the things you consider to be most important to you in your work and personal life? If you're struggling to identify these, take an online values questionnaire.

- **What are your superpowers?** What are the skills you have that you perhaps take for granted, yet are super valuable? Are you highly organized? Can you write extremely succinctly? Are you a brilliant communicator? Do you pay extreme attention to detail? If you can't spot your own superpowers, ask a friend or colleague to help identify them.

- **What other job roles or career paths combine both?** Where can you see opportunities that fulfil both your values and make use of your superpowers? It may require some research, however make use of your network and tap into contacts to learn about career options you may not have previously explored.

GETTING READY TO TAKE THE LEAP

Preparing yourself financially to make a career change is one way to look after both your financial wellbeing and the health of your bank account. Rather than handing in your notice without a plan, explore whether you can reduce your working hours in your current role to free up time to build up relevant experience through volunteering or retraining; or consider taking a part-time role to support yourself financially while you pivot your career. When it comes to managing money, there are a number of simple steps you can take ahead of making a career move. By thinking ahead about your finances, you can reduce the financial pressure that a career change might bring and avoid swapping career stress for financial worries.

1. BUILD AN EMERGENCY FUND
Before you hand in your notice and wave goodbye to your boss, turn your attention to building an emergency fund that will cover at least three to six months of living expenses. Work out how much money you need to have in your bank account each

month to cover your non-negotiable expenses, such as your housing costs and utility bills. Knowing that you have enough to cover the basics financially will free up your mental capacity to handle any other stress that comes with a job change.

Although saving your emergency fund as soon as possible may be a priority, keep one eye on your long-term savings if you can. Keep paying into your workplace pension during your employment, as this will help continue to build your financial security for the future. You might need to adjust your savings plan for a short while to build that fund; however, look for other areas where you can save a little more before you turn to your retirement contributions. Future you will thank you later.

2. REVIEW YOUR EXPENSES

A change in financial circumstances is the perfect time to spring clean your finances and take a look at where your money goes. Especially if you haven't reviewed your expenses recently, there's a fair chance you'll be paying for things you no longer want or need, whether that's a streaming platform you forgot about, or a delivery box you once signed up for. Taking the time to review your spending will help increase your awareness of what you spend and allow you to identify whether there are any areas where you can reassess your budget and save a little extra.

In the run-up to leaving her law firm role, Annie prepared to take a significant pay cut by reviewing her expenses and looking at what an average role in the charity sector pays to determine whether she could make it work financially. She says, "I did a budget where I was like, if I strip everything back, what's the least money I can earn? And it was roughly what this kind of charity sector jobs were. So I thought it's not ideal that I drop all the way back down to that, but I would love to do something that I know I'll care a lot more about, and I know that I can pay my bills if I do this."

3. NEGOTIATE YOUR ESSENTIALS

However much you streamline your spending, there are essentials that you'll still need to pay for – I'm talking about housing, utility bills, insurance and food shopping. The upside is that even with your essential spending, you can look for ways to reduce your costs and save some extra cash. When it comes to bills such as utilities, if you don't ask, you often don't get the best deal going. Make a list of all the essential contracts you're currently tied into for utilities and necessities – think internet, phone contracts, contents insurance, car insurance – and put a reminder in your calendar one or two months before your existing contract expires. When you hit the date, call up your provider and negotiate the price of your package. Research competitor deals first, so you have an idea of what you could pay elsewhere and often you'll find that your existing provider will match the deal. It's a quick and simple phone call, but plenty of people neglect to ask and find themselves paying over the odds.

Don't forget to ask your current or future employer about any employee benefits too. Depending on the direction you plan to go with your career, lots of companies offer valuable benefits which can save you money, whether that's access to a physiotherapist through health insurance, or services such as free financial advice through work.

4. COMMUNICATE YOUR PLANS

Changing careers can be overwhelming and taking a pay cut to switch directions is often challenging emotionally as well as financially. It's natural for you to question your decision, especially when those around you seem to be flying ahead in their careers. Firstly, remember that your career – and life more generally – isn't a race, and you aren't in a rush. Open up to your friends and family about your plans, your motivation and excitement around your future. That way, plans can be adjusted to fit your financial circumstances and hopefully you can find the support you need to stick to your guns on a new adventure. If those around you aren't supportive of your plans, don't be afraid to set boundaries and seek out new connections who can cheer you on. Try joining networking groups online or in real life and expand your circles.

MAKING YOUR JOB WORK FOR YOU

Career change may be the number one choice for many people, but even if you don't feel like your current work situation fills up your cup then leaving your existing job and changing career direction isn't always an option for multiple reasons. For lots of people, opting for a big career change can mean going back to education to retrain, or stepping sideways into a role that pays less than your current salary to build up your skills and experience in a new field. The good news is that staying put for the time being doesn't have to mean getting in a financial rut.

HOW TO NEGOTIATE YOUR COMP

Whether you're in a job you love or you're working as a means to an end, negotiating is a skill that everyone can learn and benefit from. It's not uncommon to tell yourself that you're a bad negotiator or that it'll never work for you; the truth is that you need to learn, practise and perfect the art. Especially when we're talking about salary negotiations, the prospect of putting our cards on the table can feel far outside our comfort zone, but the old adage is true: if you don't ask then you definitely won't get. Know how to prepare yourself ahead of a negotiation and give yourself the best shot at leaving the negotiating table happy.

- **Keep a note of your successes, big and small.** Rather than viewing a negotiation as a one-off event, start thinking about every week or month as part of the process, preparing yourself to put a strong case forward at the negotiating table. Keeping track of your achievements is one way to get ahead and be prepared for a negotiation. Start noting down all your achievements in your job, including any positive feedback that shows off your skills. Every week, set aside ten minutes to update your note and save it for any time you need a confidence boost, as well as evidence next time you have to negotiate.

- **Research is your secret sauce in a negotiation.** Make the most of the information available online and within your network to find out what other people in comparable roles are paid. Websites such as GlassDoor collect anonymous data about jobs including valuable salary insights to help inform other prospective job candidates, but don't forget to tap into the collective power of your existing contacts. If you have work friends, speak to your colleagues to gather information about what they earn; remember that by opening up about your pay and packages among yourselves, you can all benefit individually from the knowledge of whether you are being paid fairly or not. Even if you have no plans to move, tap in to the world of recruiters to find out what competitors offer and use these details as leverage when you put forward your compensation request.

- **Don't be afraid of change.** Although you can negotiate in your current role, the chances of receiving a significant increase in your compensation package will be higher if you're ready to switch companies and move elsewhere. The prospect of changing employers can be daunting, especially if you have worked in the same organization for a long time, but let the fear of the unknown get in the way and you can miss out on a world of opportunities and salary potential. Increasingly, workers are planning ahead when it comes to stepping up the salary ladder. A study by Tiger Recruitment found that 43 per cent of employees plan to change jobs within a year, with only one in five planning to stay in their current role during the same period.[8]

- **Prepare, prepare, prepare.** Whatever your situation, whether you plan to negotiate with your existing employer or you've got a new offer on the table, preparation is your best friend. Walk through the negotiation scenario in your head in advance and flip your perspective. Here's a reality check: whatever the reason why you want a better compensation package – whether it's to improve your lifestyle, pay off debt more quickly or get you closer to your savings goals – your employer frankly isn't interested. Your employer cares about one thing: how much value you bring to the company you work for, so centre the focus of the conversation on the value you add to your workplace if you want to give yourself the best possible shot of walking away happy.

CLOSING THE GENDER NEGOTIATION GAP

While encouraging women to negotiate compensation is an absolute must for boosting female salaries and closing the gender pay gap, negotiation isn't quite as simple as putting theory into practice. It might not be surprising to hear that the way negotiations play out differs significantly between men and women; gender disparities frequently surface in salary negotiations, which can contribute to reinforcing the gender pay gap.

In one study that looked at how women and men negotiate in the same scenario, even though both men and women started out with similar salary aspirations, the women advocating for themselves conceded more quickly than the men did.[9] The main reason for the concession was that women anticipated more backlash than men. In other words, women conceded more quickly because asking for more money goes against the stereotypical expectations of women in the workplace. In negotiating, women anticipated a potential negative response to their behaviour from hiring managers, leading them to settle for an offer significantly lower than the men did.

This anticipated backlash is a commonly cited reason in studies looking at the existence of a gender gap during pay negotiations. The challenge for female negotiators is that backlash isn't often clear or intentional, because if it were, it would be skirting on the edge of sex discrimination. More often than not, it's unconscious and so puts women in the position of wondering how on earth to behave. While you might not be able to change the unconscious bias toward women who negotiate that exists as a result of thousands of years of embedded gender roles in society, you can control how you approach each negotiation.

STATE YOUR CASE CLEARLY

Here is a quick checklist to help you prepare for your next salary negotiation:

- If you've had a negative experience of negotiation previously, take time to revisit the scenario and look for areas that you can improve next time.

- Practise a negotiation scenario with a friend or family member ahead of time to prepare for any curveball questions and to iron out your nerves.

- Discuss negotiation tactics with your colleagues where possible, so you can share experiences and tips with each other.

- Consider whether there are ways to influence change on a bigger scale across your organization or company, for example, by advocating for more transparent pay and compensation structures that seek to level the playing field.

One thing that's for certain is that the meaning, motivation and purpose of our work for each one of us will change, morph and shift throughout our lives. As we grow as individuals, follow our passions and set our sights on new priorities and goals over the years, our relationship with work will inevitably move through seasons. Perhaps you're in a rut right now and sense a career crossroads is coming up, or maybe you've found your stride in your job; wherever you find yourself, the future is full of opportunity. Keep in mind that we spend the majority of our waking hours earning a living, so allow yourself to change your focus and switch direction. For some, work will be simply a means to an end, while for others, finding purpose at work will be the end goal. All in all, I'm a believer that the key to a good work life is figuring out what works for you.

FOR LOVE
OR MONEY

②

My first profile name on MySpace in the early 2000s gave a good indication of how 13-year-old Ellie viewed her place in the world: princess elle. As a child born and raised in the 1990s and 2000s, I grew up on a hardcore diet of Disney heroines and happily-ever-afters. From a young age, I dreamed of my wedding day; the day when I'd finally get my ballgown moment walking down the church aisle. I'd spent years imagining the second when the surprise choir would pop up from the church gallery singing "All You Need Is Love", exactly like the scene in the movie *Love Actually*. I spent hours in my bedroom getting my Barbie dolls ready for their weddings and I had a serious obsession with the late Princess Diana, so much so that I insisted on a day trip to Althorp House to visit her resting place shortly after her tragic death. I was five years old.

Is it any surprise, then, that I took it as given that one day I would have my very own fairy-tale wedding in a grand castle, with a handsome prince? The romanticism of the fairy tale was so ingrained in my mind that, by the time I started dating in my teenage years, I already had a long list of non-negotiables for my future bridal self and a firm expectation that one day, I'd be swept off my feet, Cinderella-style.

Yet at the same time, as I imagined my future wedding day, I never really pictured myself as a kept woman. The idea of being a housewife never once entered my mind as a teenager, and work is something I never considered could be optional. This was, most likely, the result of being raised by an incredibly hard-working single mother. I've always been determined to stand on my own two feet and make my own money. I never wanted to depend on anyone else financially; I've seen how trusting someone with your money can backfire and for most of my 20s I maintained that a joint bank account wasn't for me. Now, I can comfortably look back and say that my teenage self had no clue as to how complex the world of money and relationships would turn out to be. From deciding who pays on a first date, to the financial perils of having a saviour complex, or whether engagement rings conflict with the progress of gender equality, love really is one of the biggest minefields when it comes to money. So where do we begin?

DATING UP AND DATING DOWN

Dating in the modern world isn't an easy ride. Gone are the days where you'd meet a decent prospective partner at a bar on a Friday night; someone who would make you laugh and ask politely for your phone number, with you knowing little more than his name. Meanwhile, location-flexible working has called time on any hopes of an office romance. Dating on apps, love it or loathe it, is firmly here to stay, and with that comes a whole host of considerations and options that never even entered the minds of previous generations. That's not to say that there weren't challenges to dating in the pre-Bumble and Hinge world, but dating tended to rely a lot more on who you knew and where you went, meaning that your options were somewhat limited, or, at least, weren't limitless.

These days, access to new potential partners at the tap of a finger can make the options seem truly endless (although I am very much aware that a vast number of said options aren't, well, options, but you get the gist). Along with this seemingly uncapped supply of new faces to swipe right or left on, we also have more data available at the touch of a button than ever before. Additional information can be helpful when you're dating, because no one wants to find out they've spent weeks messaging someone with totally conflicting political views. But how much data do we really need to decide whether we even want to engage in a conversation with a potential partner?

Along with carefully selected photos, witty answers to prompts and their height (exaggerated or not), occupation sits right up at the top of a dating profile, next to location. Yes, that's right: occupation. People looking for their future spouse are now given the opportunity to filter out dating prospects based on their career choice, among other things, before even saying hello or finishing scrolling through their painstakingly curated pictures. Crazy as it seems, maybe this is just a minor thing. Surely people don't swipe left or right based on occupation – do they?

The answer is a firm "yes". But before making any judgements or drawing conclusions, hold fire for a second. For millennials and Gen Z who came of age in the 2000s and 2010s, dating and finding a life partner looks a lot different to the picture of our lives we envisaged growing up in the 1990s. Rewind just 30 years, and having any sort of romantic life – before the time of hyper-connection and mobile communication – revolved around set-in-stone meeting locations and landline phone call slots bargained over with parents. Oh, how times have changed. That relatively straightforward trajectory is long gone, replaced with what feels like a long list of "traditional" adulting milestones moving further into the distance, as a result of the increasingly expensive and hostile economic environment in which we live. In a landscape in which adults in professional careers and earning objectively high wages find it near impossible to get on the housing ladder, or to fund a wedding without parental support, is it any surprise that a well-paid occupation does make someone more attractive to date?

"I'm in my 30s, I run my own business and I want a family in the future, so it's more important for me to consider a financially secure partner than in my 20s," explains Jess, 34, from southwest London. She continues, "In my 20s, I was strong-headed and determined to be financially independent, but there has been a shift in the last few years. I'm more aware now of what I want – or need – financially in a partner." So how does this play out practically when swiping left and right through dating profiles, I wonder. She replies, "If there's no career listed on their profile, I swipe past them. I want to know what career someone has now if I'm dating them; with online dating you can only work with what you see. First impressions count and there are jobs or occupations that I swipe past too. Jobs which I perceive to have a ceiling are often a no-go, as well as pilots and jobs with regular travel – it's often a gateway to cheating." And it seems like Jess is not alone.

Dating app Tinder revealed that in the UK, the list of the most right-swiped jobs on the platform for men featured more high-earning roles than on the women's list, with finance director and pilot included in the top 10. In contrast, highly paid careers didn't score more swipes for women, with the most right-swiped female jobs in the UK including nurses, teachers and cabin crew.[1] Yet while there's no guarantee that a specific income requirement will get you closer to finding love, finding a level of financial compatibility is key to a long-lasting relationship. With one in five couples identifying money as the greatest challenge in their relationship, being able to communicate calmly and clearly about money – regardless of your relative incomes – is key to both relationship and financial success.[2] So how do you start off on the right foot when it comes to communicating about money?

Firstly, keep in mind that you don't have to agree on every-thing, nor do you both have to be spenders or savers. Instead, having a clear understanding of each other's perspectives, financial priorities and goals can help you better navigate differences of opinion. Set aside time to get clear on your shared financial goals and visions, so you both feel that you're working toward a common goal. The approach you each take to reach the goal may differ, yet the reassurance that you are moving in the same direction can encourage you to stay focused on the positives rather than the differences in attitudes toward money. Finally, acknowledge that there isn't always a right or wrong way to handle money. Each individual has a unique perspective and experience of money, predominantly formed by their childhood and early years, so it's easy to view any approach that varies from our own view as incorrect. Rather, use the opportunity to learn from each other and open up about your feelings toward spending, saving and other financial topics.

TO SPLIT OR NOT TO SPLIT?

Not all that long ago, the idea of splitting the bill on a first date was unheard of. Until the middle of the last century, men were held to be the providers, so if a man didn't pick up the bill on date one, then what hope was there for your future? It made sense that back in the days when women stayed at home raising their children, they'd prioritize finding a partner who could comfortably and willingly spend money on the family. After all, if you didn't have your own income, a generous man is the least you'd look for in a life partner and potential father of your children. But we're not in those times any more. Today, the gap between male and female employment rates is the lowest since records began, changing the considerations of both genders when it comes to providing and contributing financially.

Many women don't want to feel as though they owe men anything. Whether it's explicit or not, there's often a feeling for women who are dating that if the man picks up the bill, it sets expectations for another date, or worse, it may give the impression that he is owed something sexually. Now don't get me wrong – this isn't at all to say that this is an accurate reflection of what men actually think. In fact, when I spoke about this idea to my male friends, most of them were shocked by the idea that picking up the bill could be seen as anything other than a well-intentioned offer. Rob has just turned 30; I ask him about his approach to dating and who should pay the bill. "I will always pay all of the first date, and probably up to date three," he says firmly. After speaking to many women on the topic who prefer to split the bill, I asked why he wants to pick up the bill. He explains, "I think a girl should come away from a first date feeling like a princess, regardless of whether she likes me romantically or not."

Romantic or not, it seems that not all women want to be treated to dinner or drinks on a first date. In an Instagram poll asking whether women prefer to split the bill or for a man to pick up the tab on a first date, over 900 people answered, with 64 per cent of women preferring to split. For James, an operations director living in Surrey, offering to pay the full amount is the normal course of events, but in the hope that his date will offer to split: "The hoping to split is not due to me being tight-fisted, but more because I hope she wants to split as well. I would like to split everything and hope my other half would too."

If one thing is clear, it's that it's very much up for grabs who should pay on a first date. There are still women who do want a man to pay on a first date and although more women want to build their careers, there are other women who do want to find a partner who can financially support a family. Ultimately, the best approach to dealing with the question is clear communication, so if you prefer to split the bill then make it clear from the get-go how you'd like to deal with money and avoid any awkwardness. Alternatively, if your date insists on paying and you'd like to see them again, offer to organize and pay for the next date up front. Whatever your approach, the best thing you can do is be clear with your date.

But once you've navigated the Wild West of dating in the 21st century and found a partner you can see yourself growing old with, you'd be forgiven for thinking the awkward conversations about money would become a thing of the past. In reality, the nuances and tricky situations that come with money are only just starting. From whether you go full-blown romantic gesture on Valentine's Day or keep celebrations on the down-low, there are countless occasions where the topic of money rears its head. Regardless of whether you're a grand gestures girl or a low-key kind of lady, setting expectations with your partner is the best way to ensure you avoid disappointment or embarrassment. It's not always easy to anticipate how your partner will react to occasions, so the sooner you broach the topic of how you like to handle gifts and, even better, set a budget to manage spending expectations, the less likely it is that money causes stress when special dates roll around. The upside is that once you settle into a groove of paying for joint activities and you both know what your expectations are, the initial months or years of a relationship can run smoothly, so much so that money can slip to the back of your mind . . . until the topic of rings comes up.

Before we dive into the minefield that is marriage in the modern world, it's helpful to set the scene about the state of marriage in the 21st century. There's no denying that marriage rates have fallen significantly, with the proportion of adults who have never married or entered into a civil partnership increasing between 2011 and 2021, particularly among 25- to 35-year-olds.[3] The reasons for the shift away from marriage are wide-ranging too. From the disappearance of social pressure to marry in modern society, to the spiralling cost of weddings in a climate where young people in particular are already struggling financially, having a wedding is becoming less and less common.

Yet although societal expectation has changed, the legal status of a married couple compared to a cohabiting couple is often overlooked. While on paper the only difference between two couples may be status, the financial protection afforded to couples outside of marriage or civil partnership is non-existent. The idea of common law marriage is a myth in the UK, with unmarried partners believing they have rights only to find themselves extremely vulnerable financially in the case of a separation. The situation is much the same in the vast majority of US states too, with only a very small number recognizing common law marriage, which leaves most citizens requiring a legal marriage to protect their rights. The myth of common law marriage is particularly problematic where one partner has given up work to raise children – most often the woman in a heterosexual couple, who can end up with little to no financial security in the event of a split.

Although increasingly there is pressure on governments to address this growing group of individuals, there's no sign of change on the horizon and so it remains in the hands of each couple to put in place relevant protections if you do choose to steer clear of marriage or civil partnership. A cohabitation agreement can protect the legal rights of unmarried couples, clearly setting out your intentions in the event of a separation in respect of finances, property and children, so it's worthwhile investing in legal advice if you do find yourself in this position.

ARE DIAMONDS STILL A GIRL'S BEST FRIEND?

It goes without saying that the word "feminist" is something of a controversial term these days. Vocally identifying as a feminist is laden with connotations about what you believe, who in society you align yourself with, and where you draw your boundaries. However, at its core, feminism started out as a movement for gender equality and I, for one, believe that women should have equal rights and opportunities to those that men have. We may have made progress when we compare today's society to the 1950s, but we're a long way from reaching a state even vaguely approximating real equality, especially when it comes to parity of earnings, wealth and prosperity. Yet there's a specific area where I find myself experiencing cognitive dissonance, and that is the marriage proposal. There's one question that seems to crop up in my mind time and time again, which I just cannot shake: is it anti-feminist to want an engagement ring?

Before I dive into this maze of a topic, I'm going to give full disclosure: my now-husband funded the engagement ring I wear entirely by himself. I'm highlighting this fact purely because I anticipate that a lot of people will disagree with this course of events. As with many things in the modern world of love and dating, it feels as though there can be a little bit of an ideological conflict around purchasing an expensive piece of jewellery. If we believe and advocate for equal relationships, how can we be on board with the idea that a man should save up his money and present a ring to a woman, once used to symbolize male ownership of a woman? It's a question which many women find themselves caught up on. Shona is 37 and lives in Devon with her husband and two young children. Explaining her complicated thoughts on engagement rings, she tells me, "I have one, but I should hate them. I think symbolically and historically they are hugely anti-feminist. Even the whole getting down on one knee, it's all so sexist and feeds into the idea of 'catching' a woman. But it seems the majority of girls want a whacking great expensive ring, big romantic gestures, their partner down on one knee and all that. I can't deny that I'm susceptible to the rhetoric – I was proposed to in the castle at Disneyland for crying out loud, and it was lovely. But it's unfeminist as hell!"

Is there a world in which engagement rings and feminism can exist alongside each other, or are they fundamentally mutually exclusive? At the core of the question is what you believe about engagement rings and their role in modern society. Do you see them as a symbol of ownership, used by men to mark their territory or, rather, are they a romantic tradition that once had patriarchal connotations but today is simply a pretty piece of jewellery that you (hopefully) like? The upside to the whole debate is that in the Western world at least, there isn't just one cookie-cutter way to do things any more. You really can decide what expectations you have around engagement as a couple, although remember to actually communicate your ideas with your partner rather than expecting them to read your mind.

Another reality is that the order of traditional relationship milestones has changed significantly in the last few decades, with nearly nine in ten couples in the UK now living together before marriage, and three-quarters of recent marriages in the USA preceded by cohabitation.[4] Cohabiting typically brings a level of combined financial responsibility that wasn't a factor for couples in the days when marriage was a precursor to living together, with shared bills and rent payments to make. For a couple living together with any level of awareness about each other's income and expenditure, it's all the more difficult for one partner to secretly save up for an engagement ring without the other partner noticing a gaping financial hole. This shift in living arrangements is one reason why there has been a rise in the number of couples choosing to share the cost of an engagement ring. After all, if you're crystal clear on the ring you want and you know that the ideal ring will cost a hefty amount of cash, splitting the cost of a ring can speed up the saving process and avoid some awkward assumptions about missing money.

Another approach on the rise is skipping over engagement rings altogether. With the financial pressure constantly turning up the dial on the aspirations and future goals of 20- and 30-somethings across the country, lots of couples are choosing to get engaged without a ring and, instead, committing the money to the day itself or to wedding rings. Whatever side of the line you fall on, ring or no ring, it feels as though we're heading toward a time when there really isn't a right or a wrong way to get engaged; it's all about what works for you.

THE ONE SCENARIO DISNEY DIDN'T COVER

What seems clear is that there's a historical gender divide when it comes to the expectations and responsibilities in the world of dating and love; one that in many ways is still prevalent today, whether we, as a society, are trying to move away from the traditional gender roles or not. But what happens when you take the traditional roles out of the picture – which are, of course, based on heterosexual relationships – and find yourself in a same-sex relationship? There isn't a Disney-style script which dictates how this plays out, so how on earth do you navigate conversations about money with your partner when you don't have societal expectations nudging you one way or the other?

Sophie is engaged to her partner, Nikki. Sophie dated men until her early 20s, at which point she realized and embraced the fact that she was bisexual. Over a coffee and croissant, I ask Sophie about her romantic history and whether there's a notable difference in her approach to dating men and women. She explains, "Dating women is totally different. Dating men, you look for ambition and have in mind that you want someone who will take care of you. With women, chemistry comes first and humour too – money isn't really a factor." I press Sophie on what this means in practice, and why dating men and women varies when it comes to money and finances. "It's far easier to follow the norms with money in heterosexual relationships," she says. "Dating women, every decision you make – about your careers, how you get engaged, who will stay at home with the kids – it's all an active decision, because there's no blueprint to follow so we speak about money all of the time. With men, often it's assumed how things will go because it's what society expects."

Sophie provides a much-needed reality check about gender stereotypes and our expectations, underlining that there are still so many long-standing assumptions we make in relationships. Even with an increasing number of heterosexual women preferring to split the bill on a first date, how many would propose to their partner rather than expect a proposal from a man? Maybe certain gender norms are shifting, but we're a long way from seeing real role reversal take place. Yet one thing that is clear is that women are more determined to stay in control of their money than ever before. So here's a question to ask yourself: how do you feel about the level of control you have over your finances?

MONEY, LOVE AND YOU . . .

Here are some questions to reflect on:

- How have you split financial management responsibilities in past relationships?

- In your current or most recent relationship, did gender stereotypical roles emerge around money management and financial decisions?

- Has your approach to managing finances in a relationship changed over the years? If yes, how has it changed and why?

- Are you comfortable with how you currently manage your finances alone and in a relationship?

- Is there any aspect of how you handle money with a partner that you would like to change? If so, what is it and how can you implement the change?

WHAT'S MINE IS . . . MINE

Faced with a whole host of financial challenges, the younger generations of adults are questioning a lot of the status quo – and the old assumption that couples combine finances is no different. A shift toward female financial independence is emerging, with almost one in three women aged 16 to 34 not holding any assets with their partner, compared to 26 per cent of women aged 55 and over. One of the reasons women are more likely than ever to keep their finances separate from those of their partner is the increase in awareness of issues relating to coercive control and the danger of financial abuse. Financial abuse can be difficult to identify. It was rife in times when women had no financial independence and relied solely on their partners for money. Still today, millions of women suffer from financial abuse, having their access to money controlled by a partner, and perhaps it's thanks to the increased conversation and signposting of this form of abuse that more women are choosing to keep their own money to themselves, partner or not.

There are endless heart-breaking cases of women suffering from economic abuse and although it might seem as though frank conversations about money are increasing, there's still a long way to go. Financial literacy plays a huge role in the ability to make the best financial decisions for your circumstances and it seems that poor female financial literacy, along with the fear of ending up financially tied into a relationship, has led to a decline in women opting to use joint bank accounts, both before and after marriage.

I used to be anti-joint accounts, as it goes. Having seen the financial consequences of a divorce play out during my teenage years, I took the firm stance that I would always maintain complete financial independence from any future partner. Bills split equally, no joint tenancy and definitely no joint bank accounts. This approach actually worked out pretty well for a while, and it helped me to avoid a bad situation becoming a disastrous one. In my early 20s, I found myself in a relationship where I was the higher earner. I ended up bailing out my partner on several occasions, with the relationship ultimately costing me a lot – both emotionally and financially. As the relationship fell apart, I had to cut my losses, accepting that I would never see several thousand pounds ever again and ultimately being grateful that I didn't tie myself into the relationship any further than I did. Bullet dodged.

But fast forward to the next relationship I found myself in with my now-husband, and eventually I experienced my perspective on everything 'joint' being challenged. For the first couple of years, we lived separately and we managed our own money independently, although we often talked about the future and what that might look like together. We kept things very neatly divided, splitting food shopping and dates as well as setting budgets for Christmas presents. Throughout these years, I talked openly about my concerns and my belief in maintaining financial independence, but the more we talked about money and our own experiences – from our parents' relationships with money to our own aspirations – the more I found myself questioning my commitment to keeping all our finances separate. If we wanted to build a life together, wasn't there a disconnect between our shared ambitions and keeping our money to ourselves? And if I wanted to pursue my own career goals, which involved taking a significant income hit, how would that work while my partner continued to climb the ladder in his career?

The idea of remaining financially independent has the best intentions, and it can certainly be a positive decision for some couples. That being said, there's also a reality in which it can become highly impractical for couples and there can be a whole host of situations where operating on separate financial islands can cause more harm than good. Take the scenario where you may decide to have children and one partner takes a financial hit for parental leave, how will the partner going to work avoid resentment for being the sole earner? And vice versa – what if the partner staying at home resents a loss of financial independence and needing to rely on the working partner for money? What happens if one of you decides to start a business and your income disappears for a year or two while you find your feet? Do you have to make all your joint decisions based on the lower earner, even if the higher earner is happy to cover the cost, to maintain independence? And if so, how do you avoid the higher earner feeling restricted and frustrated with their inability to enjoy the fruits of their work? The potential questions are endless.

I found myself wondering whether, collectively, we are overlooking an alternative danger in the pursuit of protecting our full independence. Romantic relationships and partnerships are intended to be what they say on the tin: working together. The statistics make it impossible to be naive about all marriages lasting, but still, more marriages do succeed than fail and a key ingredient to long-term relationship success seems to be transparency both ways. With that in mind, I can't help but wonder what the lasting impact of running independent financial lives is on any relationship, and whether we may be running the risk of being blinded by the desire for independence without full consideration of the pitfalls. Maybe financial autonomy makes untangling your lives easier but just because the statistics suggest it might happen, are we forgetting to play the odds of a lasting relationship in our favour?

All this is to say that it's still wide open for debate as to whether keeping your finances separate from your partner in a long-term, committed relationship is the best path toward a lasting relationship and autonomy over your money. Isn't what we actually want to be in a transparent, open and honest financial partnership? Call me idealistic, but I'm sticking to my belief that there are better ways to protect yourself and your relationship than hiding money from the person you share a bed with each night. Combining finances in a relationship can be visualized on a spectrum, from fully integrated to fully separate, and there's no single approach that works best. As with all things money, every person and couple is unique, so figuring out where on the spectrum works best for you both and how to make your financial management work in a practical way is important to establish.

Of course, there are ways to work together collaboratively as a couple and still maintain full control over your finances.

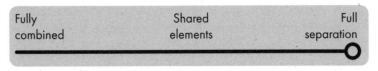

THE SLIDING SCALE OF RELATIONSHIP SHARED FINANCES

Here, strong communication is vital and transparency is needed to make sure that both partners feel that they are working together as a team, rather than two individuals. Regularly checking in about your circumstances and how you divide financial responsibilities is essential, so prioritize regular time in the diary to sit down and review. Even if you do choose to combine finances, keeping an open line of communication about how you use your money is key to avoiding conflict about spending decisions.

You may have noticed that regardless of the practical approach you choose to take to managing money in a relationship, there is one common thread that runs throughout. The level of comfort – or discomfort – we feel discussing the intimate details about our financial lives can be deeply rooted in our culture, with attitudes toward baring all varying across the globe.[5] In a 2018 survey of couples divorcing in the UK, one of the main reasons cited for the breakdown of the relationship was money, or, more specifically, a lack of communication about finances. The situation is the same in the US, with financial troubles high in the top ten reasons for marital breakdown. It seems that – much like the other reasons often listed for relationships failing – communication ultimately makes and breaks our love lives. Mismatched expectations, secret bank accounts, misaligned financial goals – they all come back to the same issue of communication.

HOW TO TALK ABOUT MONEY IN LOVE

One of the reasons that money becomes a problem in relationships is that, for many of us, it's not a comfortable topic to talk about. British culture, for example, has shied away from talking about money historically, with a whole host of reasons listed as to why we should dodge the conversation. Yet in love, more than in any other area of our lives, talking about money can truly make or break a relationship.

Whether you're team pay-your-own-way on a date or you firmly believe that paying on the first date is a duty, there's one thing to keep front of mind if you want to avoid awkward assumptions, and that's communication. It might sound obvious, but it really is true when it comes to avoiding disputes about money with a partner. Every one of us has our own views on the right or wrong way to manage money, but the key to making sure that it doesn't ruin your relationship is understanding that your date or your partner might not have the same beliefs about money as you. And that's totally fine. After all, it's not your job to convince them that they are wrong and you are right, or vice versa. Your ability to have a successful relationship will come down to your communication on the topic, whether you share the same views on money or not.

So where do you begin? Remember that conversations about money don't have to go from zero to laying out the intricacies of your bank account in 30 seconds.

BARING ALL . . . ABOUT MONEY

To get you started, here are some things to keep in mind when you want to bring up the topic of money for the first time:

Don't start off the conversation by being too direct

Talking about money at any stage in a relationship can be uncomfortable when you're not used to it, so think about how you want to raise the subject ahead of time. Often, bringing up a news story you've come across or an interesting podcast you've listened to which touches on the topic can be a great segue. Especially if you're early on dating and you want to test the water when talking about the topic of money, it can help to stay in neutral territory when discussing your perspectives.

Stay judgement-free

It can be a huge deal to be open about money, so even though you may not have the same views as your romantic partner, allow them to share their perspective without jumping in and imposing your own thoughts. From small differences such as whether Uber is a good use of your hard-earned cash, to bigger questions like the ethics of private education, having different opinions only becomes problematic when you lose respect for the other person's point of view. Rather than seeing different perspectives as wrongly held views that you need to correct, listen to your partner and avoid trying to "fix" them. Throughout any relationship, there are times when you'll need to be on the same page – but not every diverging viewpoint is a cause for concern and differences of opinion can often be navigated together.

Put money dates in the diary

Talking about money isn't a one-time thing and as any relationship progresses, financial circumstances will change for both partners, which is why regularly communicating about money is key to staying aligned and avoiding situations where money becomes a sticky issue. Putting time in the diary every so often to chat about your finances as a couple, both from a practical perspective and an emotional one, will give you the best chance at successfully navigating the financial challenges that a relationship can present.

ℱଛ

So is it all about love, or money? It's safe to say that love really does make the world go round ... but then again, so does money. Without a doubt, money has more of an impact on the success and failure of our romantic relationships today than ever before. With so many competing financial interests in our everyday lives, coupled with an unpredictable economic environment that makes achieving our financial goals seem increasingly distant, who you choose to date and build a life with can influence so much – from whether you become a homeowner or not, start your own family or quit the rat race to travel the world. When it comes to love in the 2020s, it seems as though sometimes it really is about the money!

I'LL BE THERE FOR YOU

3

Your friends are the family you choose for yourself. That's how the saying goes, and I've got to agree that there's a lot of truth to it. When you come to think of it, friendships have the potential to be the relationships that last the longest within our lifetimes. Longer than our romantic relationships, the relationships we have with our parents and even those we might have with children one day. And at the same time, they're often the relationships that we find ourselves in completely unintentionally, by accident. You cross paths over a sandpit at playschool and bond over a shared love of Barbie dolls, or you find your names next to each other on a seating plan for maths class before bonding over bad jokes in history class. Before you know it, you're a few years deep into a blossoming friendship and money has been an issue that, even if present, has been skirted around and left in the shadows.

When we look at how we meet and build our friends early on, is it any wonder that by the time we start to realize how vastly different the money cards we've been dealt are among friends, it can be a complete minefield to navigate and set off a lot of awkward feelings? It turns out that friendships are some of the most important – and challenging – relationships we have when it comes to talking about money.

THE BUTTERFLY EFFECT

In my own experience, friendships have turned out to be real-life examples of the butterfly effect in action. The butterfly effect is the simple idea that one small event that is seemingly minute in importance can be the catalyst for a major succession of events in your life. In the context of friendship, the butterfly effect theory means that a whole combination of factors have to align to place us in front of the people we later come to know as our friends. Unlike the biological connection to family and the intentional world of dating, our friends often end up in our lives by coincidence, appear at all ages and stages of life, and for many of us, the story of our friendships starts early on at school. The seemingly incidental moments that take place throughout our early lives combine to provide us with a group of nearest and dearest friends and it's only 10 or 20 years down the line when the theme of money truly starts to come into focus.

Looking back over my own life, the people I now call my closest friends today all came into my orbit through moments that so easily might not have happened. From the seat I chose on the first day of sixth form to the reluctant night out during a difficult time at university, or the gym class I turned up to spontaneously one evening in my first few months living in London, my most precious friendships today might never have existed had I made one marginally different decision in a fleeting moment in the past. Of course, it's not all fate and coincidence. Our parents and caregivers have a lot to answer for when it comes to our earliest relationships and the people we meet. The location of our schools has a major influence on the people we cross paths with, in terms of who we sit across the classroom from, to the social circles we find ourselves in later on in life.

With that in mind, it makes sense that house prices near desirable schools can be wildly expensive, with parents competing to buy not only a family home, but a fast track to specific social connections and a ticket to a certain way of life for their children. I can't speak for everyone, but it's safe to say that even when I was seven years old, my postcode had a huge impact on the adult I turned out to be. I was raised in an affluent village in Warwickshire, and my state primary school experience meant that I found myself surrounded by middle-class children with horse riding as a hobby. I'm sure that my surroundings influenced my view of the world and, from a young age, I wanted to be a version of successful. As a child who never struggled at school academically, with the combination of grades and middle-class aspirations that surrounded me, I set my sights on my ticket to success – attending a private school – at the tender age of ten.

Ah, yes, private school. It's undeniably a contentious topic and for good reason: study after study shows that a dispropor- tionate number of well-paid jobs are occupied by the privately educated.[1] And that's before you look at the upper echelons of the country and the profile of those that run the place, where those percentages get even higher. As a very determined ten-year-old, I realized that if I wanted to have the best shot of making it in whatever career I decided to pursue, private school would be the best bet and so I set my heart on it. My extremely hard-working mum did everything in her power to make it happen and although it wasn't easy to make it possible, I secured my place and subsequently benefited from the privilege of attending private school. Even when I swapped private education for a state grammar school to study for sixth form five years later, the location and demographic of my school meant that I firmly existed in comfortable circles, with the benefit that comes with friends and connections who have a hefty slice of financial privilege.

SPOT THE DIFFERENCE

When it comes to the early years of education, the financial and social implications of our school environment aren't always obvious. Particularly when we are young, the role money plays in our friendships can be subtly hidden in the connections we make or the doors that become more readily open to us later on in life. Yes, there might be things you observe and notice about the apparent wealth of your classmates – whether it's the swimming pool that they kept quiet about until you visited their home for the first time, or the exotic destinations they jet off to in their holidays. Yet when you're at school in your early teens, wearing the same uniform as everyone else and consumed with trying to win the attention of the same groups of boys, the relative financial situation you find yourself in compared to your friends can take a back seat in your mind.

Until university, that is for the most part. When filling in your personal statement and deciding which city has the best student nights out, I wonder how many of us thought long and hard about how wildly different our adulthood might look depending on where we chose to study. And while there's a huge amount of individual responsibility for carving out the life you want to live post-university, where you study – and who you meet during college or university – without doubt plays a part. Although the media narrative suggests that universities continue to make an increased effort to become more diverse and attract students from a wider range of socio-economic backgrounds, the simple nature of the education system in the UK means that certain universities attract a particular demographic of people. The stereotypes of specific universities aren't that far away from the reality, and where you study can quickly place you into a world where you feel like an outsider. As you enter adulthood, those financial differences that once seemed subtle and distant can start to come into focus sharply and for the first time, you can find yourself in a situation where you stand out from the crowd. In this scenario, one of two things tends to happen: you start assimilating the behaviour, mannerisms and aspirations of the majority, or you become increasingly aware of the difference in your financial circumstances and life experiences to those around you.

Growing up in inner London and attending a number of deprived state schools, Maria stood out as a gifted student. With ambitions to change the world at a young age, Maria set her sights on becoming a lawyer and secured a place at the University of Southampton to study law. When I spoke to Maria about her experience, she described the culture shock of meeting the other students on her law degree. "It definitely felt like most people on my course had gone to a grammar school, if not a private school," she told me. "In Southampton, I feel like it was quite rare if you met anyone from north of the Midlands; it mainly attracted people from the south and southeast, so I just met people from Surrey, Hampshire and Essex."

Alongside the realization that most of the students on her course had come from very comfortable backgrounds financially, attending university also put a spotlight on the glaring differences between the university experience for other students in contrast to her own. She explains: "I realized that there was a massive disparity of people who came with cars or those whose parents were paying for their degree, or those who had had a gap year or two before coming to university. And then friends who had just completely different shopping habits. For example, I remember some friends doing their weekly shop at Waitrose, and I'd never even set foot in a Waitrose."

The three or more years we spend at university can bond us tightly to the people we spend many days hungover with, share below-average student accommodation with and go through the highs and lows of university life with. But it's not always easy to know how best to manage financial situations when there are differences between how much each person can spend, so having a plan of action to manage money in group settings can help avoid awkwardness. Whether it's a house share, group dinner event or festival weekend away, planning ahead can save a lot of emotional stress and angst about costs.

HOW TO STAY SOCIAL AND SURVIVE FINANCIALLY AS A STUDENT

Here are some helpful tips for navigating the sorts of potentially tricky areas that can crop up, money-wise, when you are socializing as a student.

Assign tasks

Dividing up the responsibility for buying various items or booking transport and accommodation can ensure an even split of labour and spread out the cost among the group, so no one party takes on more of a financial hit than anyone else.

Agree an approach up front

Have a conversation to decide what your group budget is and whether you plan to shop for basics or go high end. Without a consensus on how much to spend, a simple plan can spiral wildly out of control and what should be a low-cost event can end up costing a small fortune.

Track your spending

The easiest way to stay ahead of the spending is using an app to manage group costs and work out who owes how much without fiddly maths. Try Splitwise for a free, easy-to-use option that works for all eventualities.

Keep a kitty

In lots of group scenarios, last minute spending will crop up, so having a cash kitty that includes a small amount of money from each person can prevent anyone ending up out of pocket when you need a new bottle of hand wash or extra bottle of wine, for example.

FILLING IN THE GAPING GAPS

Have you ever thought you know a friend inside out, only to find yourself trying to fill in missing blanks down the line? We grow up with our friends, muddle through the early years of adulthood and make plenty of drunken mistakes together. But occasionally years deep into a friendship, strange things start to happen which leave you asking questions you didn't know you needed to ask. I'm talking about that moment when one of your closest friends mysteriously drops into conversation that they've bought a flat, and you start doing the mental arithmetic to try to make sense of the situation. Running through the numbers, it's not unusual to find yourself at a roadblock asking yourself: how on *earth* did they afford that?

At the start of most careers, the earnings difference between entry-level jobs across industries can seem quite subtle. The novelty of having a monthly salary initially takes over and long-term financial aspirations go on the back burner. But fast forward a few years and slowly but surely, earnings disparities start to appear in even the smallest groups of friends. It's normal that choosing certain career paths and working in specific industries will pay more or pay less than others, yet no one prepares you for the impact that earning wildly different amounts of money to your friends can have on your respective lifestyles. So here's a question to mull over: do our friends owe us an explanation about how they fund their lifestyles? Or if we find ourselves as the beneficiaries of family help or inheritance, do we owe our friends the full details about how we've made any seemingly impossible financial moves possible? At the same time, is it our responsibility to tell our nearest and dearest if we're in financial difficulties and struggling to keep up with plans, so that they can adjust accordingly?

Nicola volunteers the details about her finances to her friendship circle and is equally open about asking questions to fill in the gaps. She says, "If I'm friends with someone, I feel like I can trust them. I don't hold anything back. I'm pretty candid about talking about everything. One of my friends was saying how much the property was that they were looking at. And I think I just said to her, 'How on earth are you managing to get a mortgage for that?' And then she was, like, 'Oh, because we've got this much put aside.' And I think they had a little bit of money from her partner's mom and dad, but then he's got a great job so it all added up."

One of the consequences of a lack of transparency about money with friends is the feeling that you're behind. While there's no universal timeline that we all should be working to or charting our progress against, seeing your classmates start buying property, go globetrotting and host extravagant weddings can leave you wondering how they have hundreds of thousands to spend, while you're struggling to save a couple of hundred each month. Yet when we start opening up about money – and asking our friends outright about their finances – we can swap the constant guessing game for facts and stop comparing ourselves to situations that might look worlds away from our own circumstances. Finding out that your best friend was gifted a huge deposit for an apartment might feel awkward and it isn't going to help get you closer to your savings goal, but it sure can help highlight that you're not "behind" or missing a trick. And that knowledge, I believe, can only be a good thing.

HANDLING THE GREEN-EYED MONSTER

Navigating money with your friends – even your nearest and dearest – can be a tricky task, especially when you find yourselves in starkly different financial situations. All too often, jealousy can creep in and have a detrimental effect on important relationships in our lives. What we earn can play a part in shifting the dynamics of a friendship, sometimes becoming evident in the off-hand comments made in passing, or the attitude toward certain job roles that start to emerge. Hannah met up with a school friend when the topic of salary among their mutual friends soon came up. She tells me, "I'd not seen her for a while, but she'd been at a hen do the weekend before and she'd always talk about the money they earn. A lawyer friend of hers is on £300,000 a year and that is a lot, I get that. But my friend always acts like that's a disgusting amount of money, and acts like she herself works really hard, which I'm sure she does, but sort of suggesting that her lawyer friend doesn't."

Unpacking how we feel about earnings and financial privilege among our friends can be uncomfortable. One reason is that we all – consciously or subconsciously – place differing amounts of merit on job roles or careers, and that influences our opinion on how much someone should earn. But the truth is that we live in a world where salaries aren't universally agreed by a grand panel, and pay isn't allocated based on the societal merit of a job. So does there need to be an element of acceptance about disparities in income if friendships are to flourish regardless of earnings? Hannah thinks so, saying, "I've been seeing doctors on Twitter being like, oh, but Instagramers earn this, or YouTubers earn that – I think you actually can't compare it because we're funded differently. It's a different job. And also, you're wasting your time. No one's going to set standard pay for footballers, so just get over that."

It all makes sense in principle, but in practice navigating feelings of jealousy in a friendship situation can be a minefield. Is it really possible to face jealousy toward friends head-on and stop it getting in the way of friendships for good? Integrative counsellor Hannah Smart believes that jealousy doesn't have to mean the end of a friendship. She tells me, "It absolutely is possible to stop jealousy from ruining friendships, especially where both parties are willing to acknowledge how they feel, empathize with each other and, where relevant, take responsibility for the part they might play in fostering competitive relationship dynamics. Ultimately, every situation and relationship is different." The question is, then, how can you start a conversation about your feelings and be up front with your closest friends when jealousy is creeping into the relationship? She replies, "We can never be 100 per cent sure how sharing our feelings will be received and what will be evoked in our friendships if we acknowledge feelings of jealousy. However, if you have a close friendship with plenty of openness, you may have some indication already of how these feelings will be received. When we come from a place of vulnerability, instead of blame, sharing our internal worlds can often lead to increased understanding and closeness in relationships. Sometimes, it can feel cathartic to share our feelings, regardless of how they will be received. We may even find out that we've been unconsciously communicating these feelings to our friends in other ways."

So while at times it might be tricky to put financial gaps to one side, there are a lot of benefits that nurturing healthy friendships can bring to our wellbeing. Good friends cheer you on, embrace you for who you are and build you up when you feel down. Friends are often the people we can turn to when times get tough and the support that friendship can bring when you need it can be worth far more than any amount of money can buy.

NURTURE YOUR FRIENDSHIPS FOR FREE

One of the beauties about friendship is that you rarely need to bring money into the relationship if you don't wish to; here are three ways you can nourish a friendship at no cost:

- **Spend dedicated time together.** It might sound obvious, yet in a busy world with its endless notifications, spending dedicated one-on-one time with your close friends can be priceless. Switch your phones on silent and go for a long walk to catch up.

- **Write your friend a letter.** Old school though it may be, there's something so endearing about handwritten letters and cards. At a time where words are so quick to type, popping down some thoughts on paper can light up someone's day.

- **Make an effort.** Whether you live on the other side of the road or the opposite side of the world, friendships need effort and it can be easy to let connection slip for months without being intentional. Set aside time to schedule a call or catch up regularly.

FORKS IN THE FRIENDSHIP ROAD

Even when we go to opposite ends of the country for university or find ourselves on different tracks, it's natural to assume we'll remain close friends with our oldest acquaintances throughout our adult lives. Friendship is a special category of relationship which is glued together by a combination of things. After all, there's a uniqueness to shared experiences and memories that go back decades, and our early childhood memories can never be replaced by people we meet later on in life. But it turns out that sticking close to the people we've known the longest isn't always the romantic idea that it might sound like.

However similar our upbringing may look from the outside, each group of friends contains a spectrum of individuals on their own individual life path and the choices we make about what we want our lives to look like, our values and our priorities – whether that's a high pay, passion for travel or pursuing our purpose – can be wildly different. A long-lasting friendship needs more ingredients than nostalgia and communal childhood tales, especially when the reality of adulthood hits and starts to send us in alternate directions. So what is the key to friendships that stand the test of time, and why do others start to splinter?

There are a handful of pivotal moments during a friendship when the dynamic can start to shift – for better or for worse – and, most often, either money or life events can be found at the root of these moments. Without necessarily knowing at the time, the way we navigate these moments in our own lives and the lives of our friends can determine whether our friendships really last forever. Sally Baker, award-winning therapist and author, helps clients deal with friendships through different phases of life. When I spoke to Sally to find out why women can find friendships challenging to navigate across the years, she said, "It's very difficult for women to keep a friendship for the whole of their lives because we take this complicated scenic route to come back to ourselves. And it includes loads of things; it includes dodgy boyfriends, divorce, children or fertility issues. And they're all things that we can compare ourselves to our girlfriends with. It's the pain of comparison."

There's no denying that comparison can cause a myriad of challenges, which we will be explore in depth later in chapter 4, "The Curse of Comparison", and according to Sally, it's natural for friendships to drift as we face up to the different phases of our lives from one another. Perhaps if we can start to better understand that friendships go through seasons, we can avoid losing the relationships we want to maintain and be more understanding of the ebbs and flows of friendships over the course of years. But not every friendship is made to stand the test of time.

LEARNING TO LET GO

Recently, I found myself wondering whether society has romanticized friendships to the point where we find ourselves blinded by the idea of a friendship and the backstory that ties us together, and ignore the fact that a relationship no longer has a positive role to play in our lives? As one of millions of millennial fans of the cultural phenomenon that is *Everything I Know About Love* by Dolly Alderton, I poured over the tale of friendship between the main characters along with all of the other 20-something female readers believing that if Dolly and her friends could remain best of friends through thick and thin, every friendship could – and should – last forever. But what about the relationships that don't add to our lives and turn toxic?

In many cases, working through your feelings of comparison and even jealousy to unpack them can help maintain a healthy friendship. Friendships, like all relationships, have seasons, so it's natural to go through high and low points as we all deal with different life events. There will inevitably be times when you feel closer or more distant to certain friends than during other phases. Equally, there are times when tough love will be needed between close friends, but for the most part, feeling supported and having your achievements celebrated isn't too much to expect in a true friendship. True friends will want to see you succeed – both in life and in your career – whatever that might look like.

However, not every friendship lasts for life and it's important to know when to walk away from a friendship that no longer serves you. Think about the signs that a romantic relationship is taking more than it's adding to your life; lots of the same signals can apply in a friendship too. Fractures in friendships can be caused by all sorts of reasons, but there are some red flags that could signal that it might be time to reassess the relationship as a whole.

HOW TO SPOT A RED FLAG IN A FRIENDSHIP

If a friendship becomes draining over a long period of time despite your efforts to improve things and you leave your interactions with your friend feeling bad about yourself consistently, it may be time to move on. Here are some signs to watch out for:

You give far more than you get

Friendships work in seasons and there will be times when one of you needs more support and TLC than the other, yet if you find that there's always drama and never any interest in your circumstances and life, the relationship may be unsustainable.

Spending time together is hard work

If you find yourself dreading spending time together and you leave interactions feeling drained, it may be a sign the friendship isn't working for you.

Your friendship feels competitive

It's human nature to sometimes compare ourselves to our peers, but real friends will celebrate each other's wins and cheer on one another when things are going well, as well as being there in the tough times.

※

In some cases, letting a friendship go might turn out to be the best thing for everyone involved, especially if negative feelings such as jealousy are causing the relationship to feel negative rather than bringing light and laughter to the table. I asked Sally how we can figure out whether a friendship has run its course or not. She replied, "One of the things we need to do is a bit of a spring clean with our friends. When we see friends, often there's a certain amount of alcohol consumption that goes on. So the next morning after you've seen a mate, you might think, 'God, I feel really crap and exhausted.' But if you were to unpick it, and think back over the evening, are you feeling crap cause you've drank too much cheap Prosecco, or are you feeling crap because they've just emotionally dumped on you for the whole evening and exhausted you? We need to have a bit of an awareness and alcohol cloaks that a bit because we get confused. But there's also a part of us that does know we've probably outgrown them and they've probably outgrown us. So let them go with kindness. Let them go and wish them well on their journey."

CONVERSATIONS WITH FRIENDS ABOUT MONEY

Talking about money with your friends might not be top of your to-do list, but there are good reasons to set aside awkwardness and get the conversation going. After all, we share details of our love lives with friends and help each other through tough times, so why are we so reluctant to open up about our bank balance? If you've never spoken about money with your closest friends, you may be surprised by how the conversation goes. There's no predicting what emotions might come to the surface when you first talk about money, especially if you find out things you hadn't anticipated. So often in our friendships, we fill in the unspoken gaps about each other's financial situations, yet when we actually find out the full story, it can turn out we've got it all wrong. So how do you have a conversation with your best friend about money and not feel weird about it?

First things first, try to approach the conversation without judgement or expectations. It's without doubt easier said than done – but the number one way to make sure that a conversation about money goes badly? Judgement. Especially with friends, it's easy to assume that we share the same attitudes and perspectives, but that isn't always the case – particularly if we're talking about money. Our beliefs about money shape how we view financial decisions, and it's easy to look at the choices someone else has made and judge them against our own set of beliefs as to what is right or wrong, sensible or stupid. Yet our beliefs are not universal; we all have a unique view of the "best" or "worst" ways to manage, earn and spend our money, and although we may share many common values with our friends, it's never a safe bet to assume that the way you relate to money is the same as everyone else around you.

While I'm all for a straight-up approach to talking about money, for the most part people find the prospect of laying bare their financial lives a little intimidating. However, when you have an idea of how to approach a conversation about money with friends, you can skip the awkwardness and have a constructive and friendly chat.

HOW TO START THE CONVERSATION

If you've never talked about finances with friends before, it's not advisable to plunge right in at the deep end. Rather than kicking off the conversation by asking a friend how much they earn or what their bank balance looks like, start by broaching the topic of money more broadly. Ask for their take on a recent money-related news story, for example, or share an episode of your favourite podcast that talks about earning, spending or saving. When you bring the topic of money to the table without making the conversation personal, you show your willingness to discuss money. Dive in deep right away and you run the risk of putting up your friend's guard, making them far less likely to open up to you about tricky topics. Remember that the aim of the conversation isn't to rush into airing all of your financial laundry straight away, but to build trust around a sensitive subject so that you can hopefully reap the benefits of talking about money candidly with them in the long term.

There are two ways a conversation about money with a close friend can go: either you already know the majority of what they tell you about their financial situation, or you find out something you had no clue about. Handling the first situation doesn't need an explanation, but digesting a financial bombshell that you didn't see coming can be hard and might require some tact. Simply because it's still often culturally perceived as awkward to talk openly about our finances, discovering that someone close to you is dealing with an alternate set of financial circumstances to those you imagined, based on what you thought you knew, can be a shock to the system. You might find yourself going over the past in your head, trying to reconcile what you now know to be true with the version of events you previously understood, and looking for hints that you might have missed. You're not alone if you find it tricky to wrap your head around the reality in front of you, both if you find out that a friend has a lot more financial stability – or a lot less – than you previously thought. Don't fall into the trap of judging your friend or viewing them differently based on their financial situation; being open with each other about money can feel exposing, so mutual respect is vital in open conversations with friends.

CONTROL WHAT YOU CAN

The upside is that money really doesn't have to make or break a friendship. Communication and compassion are the key ingredients to navigating friendships where your financial circumstances are worlds apart, and although it might not always be easy, it's definitely possible and can result in a long-lasting and positive relationship.

The contrast between Gemma and one of her closest friends in how they handle money hit home in a taxi ride over to her friend's house for dinner. She said, "They invited us over for dinner. I being who I am, went and bought something to bring over because I didn't want to show up empty-handed. I bought a really expensive bottle of alcohol. We get an Uber there and on the way over, I get a message saying, 'Hey, would you mind transferring me your half for dinner?' I just sat in the car and I thought, 'Is this genuine?' I thought she would've said when she invited us, 'Hey, do you mind splitting the cost before we have you over?' So it could be pre-discussed and maybe I wouldn't then bring a gift – because I've paid my way."

Once she realized that her attitude to hosting friends and finances differed hugely from her friend, Gemma adjusted her approach to dealing with money in the friendship. "Now going forward, I've realized that she does like to have people pay equal amounts for things when there's any situation," she explained. "And so I think that must just come down to how she's been brought up experiencing money – that people should cover their costs. Now I've learned that and I've come to terms with that. That's fine. That's how she is. And I love her." Awkward moments aside, Gemma's experience is testament to the fact that it is possible to navigate polar opposite approaches to spending and sharing money, as long as you communicate and show understanding to your friend's way of doing things.

TIME TO TALK MONEY

Opening up about our finances is still considered to be taboo for many, so it's no surprise that not everyone wants to drop a message into a group chat, explaining that their budget is tight right now. Practically speaking, there are several steps you can take to avoid your finances spiralling as a result of social plans. If you regularly find yourself in a situation where you feel the pressure to overspend to keep up with your friends, or you end up saying yes to fancy restaurants that blow your weekly budget just because the highest earner makes the plans, it's time to take control of the situation.

Social connection and time with our nearest and dearest are crucial to our mental wellbeing, so instead of finding yourself saying no to going out because of your budget, try to think about how you can influence the plan to make it work for you. For example, rather than waiting for your friends with expensive tastes to organize your social calendar, be the first to put a plan on the table that works for your financial situation. Whether that's a weekday restaurant deal, a free day out to a museum or hosting a potluck dinner at your flat, taking the initiative with planning can restore a sense of control over group spending, which often gets lost in social setups.

Even in scenarios where you have a fully formed plan presented to you before you've even had a chance to look at the budget, don't panic. Most of the time, we tend to make social plans based on the knowledge we have available and frequently, we jump to conclusions where we have gaps in factual knowledge. Unless you are comfortable talking about money with your friends, there's a high chance they are making guesses about how much you can or cannot afford to spend and they may well be wildly off the mark. So, yes, there might be special occasions when one of the girls is desperate to go to a brand new flashy venue, but the majority of the time? We don't make plans with our friends because we want to go to a bougie restaurant; we make plans because we want to spend quality time together and chances are, how much you do or don't spend during that time is a side note.

But it's easy to sit here and say that spending time together is what matters, not spending money. The trouble is that all too often, we let shame or embarrassment creep into our minds and stop us from being honest about our finances, choosing instead to keep quiet and deal with the consequences for our bank account later. But maybe we're underestimating our best friends? Imagine flipping the script and thinking about how you would feel if you found out that one of your friends had overspent to keep up with your plans, but they avoided telling you for fear of feeling awkward or worse, disappointing you.

After previously lending money to one of her close friends, Gemma is more conscious of the financial situations that her friends might be in. She says, "If we go out and they say, 'I'll buy this drink', I sometimes think, Should you be offering that? Are you putting yourself in a position of debt? I wouldn't want a friend to do that for me." So perhaps next time you squirm at the suggestion in your group chat to go to a high-end restaurant for dinner when you're on a tight budget, or your group holiday plans escalate out of control before you can chip in to the chat, try reminding yourself that your friends are not your number one fans because of your financial means. Yes, it might be a cliché, but when it comes to being frank with our friends about our finances then honesty really is the best policy. We can't expect our friends to read our minds and know the ins and outs of our bank accounts, but we can give them the opportunity to flex plans to work within our financial limitations by being up front and honest with them.

And if your friends aren't open to adapting plans to work with what you can afford? Well, maybe it's time to question if they really are the friends you thought they were after all.

THE CURSE OF COMPARISON

4

Have you ever picked up your phone, opened up a social media app and found yourself thinking, *I wish my life looked more like that*? Welcome to the world of comparison culture.

Before we dive into the role comparison culture plays in our lives today, let's rewind the clock a little and head back in time. Comparison isn't a new phenomenon; we humans have always compared ourselves to others to some degree or another, yet the idea of social comparison first surfaced in the 1950s. Psychologist Leon Festinger developed social comparison theory, which is the idea that people determine their own social and personal worth by looking at others and deciding how they stack up against them. Long before the emergence of Facebook, Instagram and TikTok, seeking to evaluate ourselves alongside others has been a way for humans to track and measure their progress or success.

From when we are young, comparison plays a part in how we see ourselves and perceive our place in the world we inhabit. Think back to school, where as early as our junior years we may have been ranked by our academic abilities, or by our sports talent by being placed in either the A or B team. Whether we realize it or not as children, our perception of our ability is shaped by the places that others around us occupy and reinforced by grades in a system that frequently rewards hitting top marks over individuality or uniqueness. It seems that for many, our earliest awareness of where we fit in to society in comparison to others around us is instilled long before we really become aware of it ourselves.

Alongside the influential role school plays in shaping our sense of comparison, it only takes a quick look back at pop culture during the 2000s and 2010s to see why so many millennials entered adulthood with a skewed expectation of what was to come. As I was a teenager who came of age watching *Friends* reruns on a weekly basis, it's no surprise that I expected my adult life to resemble something far more glamorous and with a lot less financial strain than the reality has turned out. I'd go as far as saying that there's a strong argument that *Friends* needs to come with a disclaimer: your 20s will categorically not involve living in a giant West Village apartment complex and hanging out with your best friends all day (unless you're a trust-fund kid with no job). Of course *Friends* isn't a reality show and dramatic licence is at play, but I'm sure that my expectations of adulthood were influenced by – and compared to – the shiny versions displayed on screen of what lay ahead.

Friends aside, it seems as though comparison has a bad reputation in the modern world. We often hear about the harmful effects of comparison, both for our mental health and from a financial angle too. But it's worth keeping in mind that comparison isn't entirely a bad thing; there can be a positive side to the instinct we have to compare ourselves to others.

Dr Sarah Bishop, a clinical psychologist, describes how we can benefit from social comparison, explaining to me: "Social comparison can be a good thing: it can motivate us to 'keep up' in the things we are striving toward. This creates a social ratchet effect, where each person's activity generates more activity among others. When we are striving toward our goals in life this can be a powerful motivator – when it's harnessed in a balanced and realistic way."[1]

Comparison can act as a powerful tool if we choose to see the achievements of others as proof of what is possible. Take sports players as an example: would world record athlete Usain Bolt ever have run 100m in 9.58 seconds if he had no other time on record to compare himself to through his years of training? The chances are extremely slim. Without any external benchmark or measure, it can be almost impossible to see what can be achieved, or to be inspired by the feats of others in a positive way.

Whether we're conscious of how we compare ourselves to others or not, money and privilege all play a huge part in our perception of our place in the world – and comparing ourselves to others is one way that we seek to establish where we fit in. So how do we stop ourselves from spending our precious lives stuck in negative comparison? And is there a way to confidently handle comparison in order to look after our own mental and financial wellbeing?

THE COMPARISON TRAP

Although comparison can serve a positive purpose in motivating us toward our individual goals, the sheer intensity of comparison in the hyper-connected world we live in can mean we sometimes need a hand to stay in our own lanes. Even though comparison isn't a new phenomenon, it feels as though we now live in a world where the comparison has intensified to a level never before seen. We spend our days plugged into the rest of the world on screens that show us a glimpse of the lives others live, but with no way of distinguishing what is real from what is fake. Which leads to the question: has the shift in the way we now live digitally influenced how much we compare ourselves and our financial situations to others? Or are we simply more aware of the negative impact comparison has on our mental and financial wellbeing?

It's worth dropping in a reminder that comparison is not unique to the digital age. Long before the millennium, glossy magazines and TV shows dominated popular culture and influenced the way people viewed themselves in society. The rich and famous were plastered on the cover of *Vogue* and *People* magazine, plus there was no shortage of photoshopped models on posters flaunting perfectly poised looks for us to try to emulate. Celebrities have existed since the dawn of time and their rock-star lifestyles have long been the envy of men and women around the world. Yet for decades, aside from the A-list celebrities who appeared on posters and screens, our circle of reference for comparison remained relatively small. We only had access to the lives of a select group of people: our friends, family and classmates or colleagues. Until the year 2004 arrived and a little-known website changed everything . . . The emergence of social networking sites and the dawn of Facebook started off the boom in comparison culture that we've experienced over the last 20 years. No longer was comparison limited to people we knew in real life; we could now compare every aspect of our lives to the version of reality that acquaintances and long-lost friends published on the internet for our consumption.

Even with the first version of a social network that was vastly different to the platforms we use today, our exposure to the life stages, successes and rare failures of others increased tenfold. Never before had it been possible to browse the luxury holiday photos of a primary school friend you last spoke to ten years ago, congratulate an acquaintance from your old netball club on becoming a CEO at 30 – or compare your own journey to the hundreds of people within your broad social network. The ability to keep up to date with the latest news that people chose to share online created a sense of intimacy and familiarity, which came hand in hand with the instinct to compare.

And then came the dawn of the influencers. In its nascent form at launch in 2010, the photo-sharing app Instagram provided a virtual curated photo experience, in which we were all encouraged to select, filter and upload our best pictures to share with a wider audience. Initially, this audience comprised our friends and family and today this remains the same for many of us. Yet for other users, strangers from further afield began to start following them in order to watch their curated, snap-happy lives from afar; and, over time, certain people started to attract a following of tens, or hundreds, of thousands of people. The image-based nature of the platform allowed followers to feel as if they were friends with the people they followed, because, after all, they knew what they wore, where they got their coffee, even where they holidayed. More often than not, these people were relatable in a way that pop stars and A-list celebrities were not. They chatted with their audience in the comments and shared information about their everyday lives that their audiences could join in with. It's no coincidence that the early movers to emerge on the scene had a combination of likeability, relatability and a sprinkling of aspiration that kept their audiences hooked – and growing in numbers. These individuals – or influencers – started to amass a huge amount of power online.

Yet the relationship between influencers and followers isn't always straightforward. One major factor behind the rise of influencers over the last decade has been the level of authenticity and reliability they provide in a manner that previously didn't exist among traditional celebrities. Influencers inhabit a world between the famous and the non-famous, dealing with the everyday trials and tribulations of life and sharing their perspectives online as though talking to their friends over coffee. But as influencers began to command bigger and bigger audiences, both they and brands soon cottoned on to the fact there was a whole new realm built on trust to explore for potential sales opportunities and to tap in to for business gain.

Audiences trusted the influencers they chose to follow, so selling products to these communities of followers proved to be incredibly effective. Brands riding the early wave of influencer marketing such as Gymshark, Lounge Underwear and Glossier saw incredible growth; so much so that today, they remain some of the most valuable companies in the UK and US. Influencers were effective marketing tools, as instead of the weeks or months typically required to warm up a new audience to a product, marketers could jump right in and sell to a warm audience straight away. The commercial value of influencers started to spiral and the money flooded into the industry, allowing influencers, who were once students living and filming their everyday lives in a relatable way, to go on holiday to the Maldives. Before we knew it, our favourite relatable internet friend started wearing new gym kit every week and eating out at the best restaurants in the city, leaving the audience – the very people who built their influence and who once felt like they could relate to them – wondering, *how on earth can they afford that*?

Cue comparison culture kicking in. The subtle intertwining of relatable and romanticized that takes place in the public profiles of influencers has led to an often confusing perception of reality online. In those moments where we consume content that seems real, untangling our personal circumstances from the apparent glamorous real lives of those we choose to follow can put our own choices, decisions and often our supposed failures under the spotlight. So here's your reminder: social media isn't real life. Whether somebody has 100 or 100,000 followers, the chances are they're not posting their everyday life in raw format for the entire world to consume. Even the moments of vulnerability or sadness that influencers choose to show are selectively uploaded to remain "real". The truth is we rarely see the full picture, but we all play the game; not often do we ourselves tell the full story when we choose to share our lives online either.

So here's a challenge for you: set aside ten minutes to scroll through your social media feeds and assess how the influencers, brands or other individuals you choose to follow impact you. Are they adding positively to your experience online? Do you feel that you learn new things or gain insights you value from following the accounts you choose to follow? Alternatively, do feelings of insecurity, negative comparison or an urge to spend rise to the surface? If any accounts set off those negative feelings, you know what to do: it's time to click unfollow or mute.

YOU CAN'T BUY HAPPINESS – OR CAN YOU?

For anyone who's ever been in a sticky financial situation that leads to stress and worry, coming across the popular quote that money can't buy happiness can feel like a real sting. The reality is that there are countless situations where money can be the answer to help improve a situation and relieve the panic or anxiety that comes with struggling to make ends meet or keep afloat financially. When you're deep in the trenches financially, listening to someone who is comfortably off tell you that money won't make you happy is likely the very last thing you want to hear. But here's the thing: there really is some truth to the saying that money can't buy happiness. There's a good reason why time and time again quotes appear from the latest round of media-savvy millionaires declaring that their six sports cars and glossy mansion don't make them happy. That reason is a little cited phenomenon that impacts us all – whether we're one day hoping to increase our bank balance by a month's salary or a lottery win – and it's called the hedonic treadmill, or *hedonic adaptation*.

The crux of the hedonic adaptation model is that when both good and bad things happen, humans tend to return to a set point of happiness and that the initial high or low experienced from changes in circumstances fades over time. Have you ever told yourself that if you only had your own house, or you just got that one more promotion, or you could go on holiday to New York just one time, you'd be happy? We've all been there, and it turns out that although those brief moments of achievement feel great, normality soon returns and we return to a level of happiness similar to that before the event happened. Take a moment to look around you at the life you live now – it might be your friendships, relationships, career, social life, fitness or anything else that comes to mind. Now cast your mind back five or ten years into the past. Do you remember a time when you dreamed of having some of those things that you do have now, which you truly believed would make you happier, yet today they feel simply part of the usual course of your life? That's hedonic adaptation in full force.

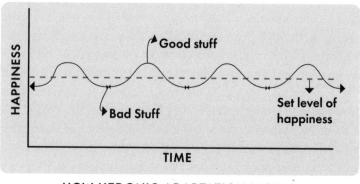

HOW HEDONIC ADAPTATION WORKS

Hedonic adaptation may be a part of human nature, so trying to get off the treadmill for good can be a challenge. On top of our own tendencies to look around and see shiny new goals or purchases we want for ourselves leading us to hop back onto the treadmill, there are whole industries working hard to tap into our endless pursuit of happiness. And selling a dream life to customers chasing every step closer to perfection and happiness they can find? It's a lucrative business.

Marketing is a force to be reckoned with. On paper, the marketing industry has a simple purpose – to sell products and services. Yet the impact of marketing on our consumption habits and mental wellbeing has shifted as the world has become more digital, with seemingly endless exposure to messages telling us that we can be happier if we just buy one more thing. There's a catch, though: there's always just one more thing. If we just buy one more dress, add that innovative new concealer to our make-up bag, or have dinner at this cool restaurant opening, we'll get closer to the elusive state of happiness. Or so we're told. That's how billion-dollar industries have been built by weaponizing comparison. It sounds complicated, but the recipe really is simple, easy to follow and has been deployed by brands across sectors from beauty to fitness, wellbeing to skincare – for huge financial gain.

With an upcoming move to the US, a person who I'm going to call Ada* found herself being drawn toward influencers selling teeth whitening and social media adverts declaring the beauty of having super-white teeth. But the tipping point came when she went to visit her lifelong dentist, who commented that her teeth would stand out in the US if she didn't get them whitened before moving. Feeling the pressure of comparison from all angles, Ada agreed to teeth whitening on the spot at a cost of £500. She tells me, "I regret spending that much money on it, and I feel I was pressured into it by my dentist, who used comparison culture to sell me a cosmetic product which was irrelevant to my oral health." The sensitivity of so many people about their appearance makes for easy exploitation of our vulnerabilities to sell a product or service. You only need to take a look at the weight loss industry to see the way comparison has been used to make millions, often at the expense of the physical, mental and financial wellbeing of the individuals looking to lose weight. The CAP (Committees of Advertising Practice) have published extensive guidelines on the use of before and after photos, along with warnings about exaggerated claims that sell people miracle solutions, yet the industry is still filled with clickbait claims that can be difficult to prove. Comparison is a strong instinct to tap in to and when you sell someone a future version of themselves, it can be a lucrative business.[2]

But comparison in marketing isn't always a bad tactic. Alice Benham, marketing strategist and podcast host, explains how marketers can use comparison without becoming problematic, telling me, "Comparison in marketing is incredibly powerful when partnered with transparency and choice. We often buy

---

* Some names have been changed for reasons of confidentiality.

things because we want to achieve a certain lifestyle, experience or result – comparison can help show us that this is possible and help us to make a choice about how we access that result." But at what point does the marketing turn sour? She says, "The time when comparison marketing becomes problematic is when there's a lack of transparency and choice, and it's often down to the messaging used. We see this when diet products use fake before and after to sell their newest fad, or pressure people to buy from a place of shame and insecurity. People's purchasing decisions should be a positive and empowering one!"

HOW TO COMBAT HEDONIC ADAPTATION

We may not be able to completely avoid the phenomenon of hedonic adaptation; however, we can build daily habits that help us to focus on boosting our happiness in small doses and appreciate what we do have. Here are three things that can help to slow down hedonic adaptation and keep your happiness levels high:

Focus on the present moment

It's easy to get swept up in chasing the next goal or target and forgetting to pause to look at where we are now; yet when we shift our focus to the present and look at what we do have that we're grateful for, our cups fill up and we feel happier with what we currently have in the moment.

Give rather than receive

Hedonic adaptation kicks in when we zone in on gaining more money, power or material possessions. But plenty of studies have shown that when we spend time helping others, whether that's through charitable giving or volunteering, our happiness levels increase.

Look inward

Easier said than done. However, we will find ourselves trapped on the hedonic treadmill when we look outward for fulfilment and gratification. By learning to look inward to ourselves for happiness rather than external markers, we can find ways to be happy regardless of our outside circumstances.

ARE WE READY TO REMOVE THE FILTERS?

Perhaps it's too early to call time on comparison culture, but there are a few signs that the coming years might see a shift away from heavily curated to authentic online. Social media is here to stay, which isn't something to be sad about; there are endless positives to the platforms we have at our fingertips. Without social media, thousands of innovative and creative businesses wouldn't exist (my business included). The harmful impact of the unrealistic expectations we place on ourselves that have sprouted from the selective view of the world we consume on social media are more widely known. And with increased awareness has come a sharper focus on how to limit the way social media consumption influences our lives, along with how comparison – both on- and offline – can cause chaos for our mental health and our financial wellbeing.

There are hints that after a decade of Kardashian-style filtered images, authenticity is the new currency online and that Gen Z in particular, born between 1997 and 2012, are seeking more reality in the content they consume. As the first generation of true digital natives, Gen Z have driven the rise of TikTok, which boomed during the pandemic, finding enjoyment in the scrappier and less edited video content favoured by the app algorithm. App developers have sought to jump on the apparent desire for more unedited social platforms too, with candid photo app BeReal soaring to popularity in 2022 and gaining momentum with users looking for a less polished social media experience. But with the ability of established social media platforms to simply add new features imitating new platforms and a hard-wired habit of using existing channels, whether or not we're ready to give up on social media as we know it in search of authenticity remains to be seen.

Advertising authorities across the world have stepped into the realm of social media in a bid to limit the covert marketing of products online, putting in place rules to ensure that influencers disclose when they are selling products for financial purposes. With the intention of clearly informing audiences that a product or service isn't a recommendation from a friend but a commercial agreement, advertising boards aimed to help consumers make more informed decisions. Yet enforcement of the rules is lax, with many major internet personalities still failing to disclose adverts in pursuit of sales figures. Plus even with disclosure, influencers often benefit from perks such as free holidays and hotel stays that everyday people can only dream of. Although advertising rules have helped to shine a light on the business of influencing, there's still a lot of comparison that comes into play.

So in a world of social media smoke and mirrors, where it's not always clear to see where the truth ends and fantasy starts, learning to accept yourself for who you are and letting go of comparison can be a squiggly journey. Yet freeing yourself from the trap of comparison really can change your life for the better, allowing you to improve your financial and mental health. For anyone aiming to break free from comparison, one of the first steps in the process is acknowledging how you feel. When you become aware of how comparison may be impacting your thoughts, behaviours and decisions, having tools at hand to help you step away from the negative thoughts can allow you to switch your perspective.

Remind yourself that the pictures you see and snapshots of successes that you hear about are often highlight reels, rather than the full picture. What we rarely see is how someone has funded their luxury holidays, the sacrifices they have made to earn a high salary or even the stress that comes with maintaining significant financial commitments. At the same time as acknowledging that you can only see others' highlights, shift your focus. "Move the focus from outward to inward," suggests behavioural change coach Gemma Perlin. "Comparison takes energy away from connecting with your identity and unique superpower of you being you. I find people focus more on the outward when they are lacking connection to their purpose. If you are really connected to what you want, what other people are doing feels less important."

HOW TO HANDLE COMPARISON

There's no pretending that it's easy to switch off from the influence of comparison culture. Fortunately, learning to stay in your own lane and reduce the negative impact of comparison on your mental health and your bank balance is possible, so here are a handful of tools to put in your anti-comparison locker.

GET CLEAR ON YOUR VALUES

There's nothing that sets off comparison more than feeling lost and unsure about what we really want from our lives. There are plenty of things we do learn during our childhood, but one thing we're rarely taught is the skill of figuring out what actually matters to us as individuals. What makes us tick. What is important to you in your life. For all the good that studying Shakespeare does, there's no guide book we get given on how to really work out our own core values. Yet when you don't know what your core values are, you're left making decisions in the dark. Not knowing what your values are can lead to a long search for happiness.

Think about the many interviews out there with highly successful business figures in which they declare that lots of money didn't make them happier. Often, they've pursued money and wealth, but only on seeing their healthy bank balance have they realized that money doesn't satisfy their instinctive human desire for fulfilment or purpose. They haven't been living in alignment with their core values.

When you do define your own values, you can then make decisions that get you closer to what matters to you, rather than pursuing the goals or milestones that society shouts about.

Take, for example, the hard-working student who follows in the footsteps of her classmates to find herself in an office job working 15-hour days on complex matters for giant global corporations. She might be earning a hefty salary, have a high-flying job title on her LinkedIn profile and spend her annual leave on exotic holidays – yet if one of her core values is altruism and she feels as though she is spending her days working to make faceless companies richer, she may find herself feeling unsatisfied and wondering why her on-paper success isn't enough. The answer is that her current way of life isn't serving her core value of altruism.

So how do you work out what your core values are? Well, there's no one-size-fits-all approach to take, but there are a few things to reflect on. It's sometimes difficult to untangle what you actually do want in your own life from what you see others have around you, especially when it comes to traditional milestones that society tends to celebrate. Emma Wilson, life coach and founder of the Turning 30 Coach, works with women in their late 20s and 30s to help them get unstuck and feel better. She says she sees the impact of comparison on a regular basis. I asked Emma how to handle comparing where you are right now to others who are perhaps where you thought you might be in your life at a specific point. "Try to separate the shoulds from the desire, which a lot of people forget to do," she advises. "If you notice that you feel yourself saying a lot of the time 'I should do this, I should do that' instead of 'that's what really lights me up and sets my soul and fire and makes me feel good', that's quite a strong indicator that you're being more affected by what other people have and less in line with what you want yourself."

When you strip back all of the distractions that we have from all angles, whether that's our friendship circles, social media networks or the stream of 24/7 marketing we're exposed to, focusing on yourself becomes easier. Emma calls this "turning up the volume on yourself", and says, "If you're constantly looking outward to other people and what other people think, say, 'I'm going to turn down the volume and make everyone else background noise and turn the volume up so high on me that it drowns out all the noises.' That can look like loads of things: from getting into a really good routine, focusing on your goals or your career, working on your mindset. It might be starting coaching, therapy, a personal development journey or finding a hobby."

It's worth remembering too that your values can shift over time. In the same way that our lives go through seasons and our priorities shift as we grow and change as individuals, not all of our values are static. So it's worthwhile revisiting and redefining your values and what sets you alight over time, as you experience new things and life turns in unexpected directions. And those times where you feel stuck or in a rut and can't figure out why? It might just be that you've slipped out of alignment with your values once again.

PRACTISE MINDFUL SPENDING

Whether you class yourself as a professional in the art of mindfulness or you struggle to switch off your brain, learning to spend intentionally is one of the best ways to keep comparison in check. With constant nudges in every direction we turn to make shiny new purchases, it can be a real challenge to stop yourself falling into the comparison trap and trying to buy your way to feeling better. Learning to spend mindfully isn't an overnight fix to any decades-long spending habits, but it has completely changed my relationship with spending money. Mindful spending isn't about stopping spending altogether, either. Similarly to mindfulness in the broader sense, the aim of mindful spending is to make more considered choices about where to spend your money – and where to save as well. When you practise mindful spending, you can disentangle yourself from the impulse to spend and avoid the post-checkout buyer's remorse that we've nearly all experienced.

The first step in becoming more conscious of your spending is by taking a bird's eye look at your spending and identifying which spending choices matter to you the most. I'm not talking about the essential expenses you have no choice over, because I'm yet to find someone who feels that their council tax bill is a worthy use of their money. Rather, review your discretionary spending and the areas where you do have the ability to make a spending decision, and ask yourself whether the way you currently spend your money is enhancing your life, or simply in pursuit of another easy purchase without thinking.

This is a highly personal process, primarily because what we value spending money on might look totally different to what others value, so it's a task best carried out on your own. All too often, our instincts about where it's worth spending more money – and where it isn't – can be clouded by the views of those around us, even if they don't reflect our own thoughts. For someone who prioritizes nutrition and food above all, organic produce and high-quality meat may be non-negotiable in their weekly shop. At the same time, you won't struggle to find a camp of people with the view that organic is a marketing buzzword and who prefer to save money by choosing cheaper food options. Being mindful about your spending doesn't mean there's a good or bad approach; it's making decisions about spending that align with your values and priorities.

INCREASE THE SPENDING FRICTION

For all the brilliant innovations and ways that technology has made our lives easier, quicker and more efficient, there's a darker side to its advancements. Never before has it been so easy to spend money without noticing, with the way we spend money becoming so frictionless and simple that we can entirely detach ourselves from the money we spend. From contactless payments to Apple Pay to One-Click checkout, long gone are the days when you had to hand over cash – or even a bank card – to pay for your purchases. On top of the payment itself, we are constantly bombarded by incentives to spend, from notifications to email newsletters and more. Helpful as it may be to save time and stay in the loop with our favourite brands, technology has dissolved the conscious steps we take to spend and made it easier than ever to spend money mindlessly.

There's a reality check here: the banking industry wants us to spend money, so there's zero likelihood that they will make it more difficult to spend money anytime soon after spending decades – and billions – to make shopping so seamless. We have to take charge and put in place steps to protect our own financial wellbeing by building friction into the purchasing process. It might seem counterintuitive in a world of instant gratification and same-day delivery, yet it's one of the simplest ways to give ourselves the valuable breathing room to make conscious spending decisions . . .

BECOME SPENDING AWARE AND BUILD IN A LITTLE FRICTION

Thinking about how exactly you can take charge and start to become a little more conscious of your spending? Here are some simple ways to boost your spending awareness:

- **Review your expenditure.** Start by taking a look at your current spending habits and then identify where the triggers are for you individually to spend mindlessly. It might be that email newsletters about the latest clothes drop are your Achilles heel; for others, it's that double-click payment on your phone which feels like free money. Once you identify where your spending vulnerabilities are, you can start to add in friction and slow down the speed of the checkout process.

- **Delete saved card details.** The ease of checking out online when you have saved card details means we no longer have to pause to consider whether we really want to go ahead with a purchase. Frustrating as it might sound, when you have to find a physical bank card and type in the details, the additional friction involved in getting up from your seat can be enough to make you pause and ask yourself whether you really want and need to make the purchase.

- **Turn off shopping app notifications.** There's a strong argument for turning off phone notifications altogether: apps are designed to hook us and hold on to our attention, so by turning off notifications you can take back control over when you use your phone. This rings especially true for shopping apps that notify you every time new stock drops. Reduce the noise and save your bank balance by hitting the notification-off button.

- **Use the wish-list feature.** Plenty of shopping apps allow you to create a wish list or favourite items list, so use the feature to your advantage and rather than clicking "add to basket" right away, pop the items you have your eye on onto the wish list. Then aim to leave the wish list alone for a period of time, whether it's two hours or 24 hours, so that by the time you return, the thrill of the purchase has gone and you can objectively decide whether or not you want to go ahead and buy the items.

THINK SUSTAINABILITY OVER SCALE

Back in the 2010s, the idea of shopping second-hand and building a pre-worn wardrobe sounded completely alien. Charity shops were associated with old, unwanted clothes that had long gone out of fashion and the words Depop and Vinted had no meaning. I'll put my hands up and admit that in my early 20s, I was a one-wear-per-dress kind of girl. It's not a consumption habit I'm proud of; however, I certainly wasn't alone. "Cheap chic" fashion hit the mainstream, with the industry slashing production lead times in half to try to keep up with demand.[3] But alongside the environmental impact of this rapid wardrobe turnover, the knock-on effect on our bank accounts was tangible.

Oh, how times have changed. Over the last decade or so, awareness of the problematic nature of fast fashion has skyrocketed. Not only has there been an increase in the collective consciousness about the sustainability of the fashion industry, the cost of keeping up with ever-changing trends has led to the revival of second-hand clothes and resale platforms. And perceptions have changed; shopping second-hand now feels like an opportunity to discover a hidden gem, or grab a bargain wardrobe staple at a fraction of the retail price. Even if you love consuming fashion content, becoming more aware of your environmental impact – as well as your bank account – can help manage that urge to click "buy now" each time a marketing email from your favourite brand drops into your inbox.

Another hack to help shift your mindset is looking at how you construct your wardrobe. Comparing your wardrobe constantly to what others are wearing is a losing game; there will always be more items to buy and the fashion industry will do its very best to convince you that you just need one more item. Every few days. Instead, why not try building a capsule wardrobe? With a solid capsule wardrobe, you'll have fewer clothes in your closet but each item will be carefully chosen to coordinate. A capsule wardrobe reduces the decision-making process every day and vitally, makes it easier to say no to the endless temptation of new clothes, as you have clear criteria about what items work within your wardrobe and what is a spontaneous one-off purchase that won't stand the test of time.

For a guide to start building a capsule wardrobe, I spoke to Kim Turkington, founder of Love Cloth and fashion blogger. Kim believes that a capsule wardrobe starts with classics. She explains, "Having a good collection of classic items that you feel great in and matches your lifestyle is the best start to any wardrobe. This could be a foundation of tailoring, knitwear, T-shirts and a great pair of jeans that will never date. (Well, that's mine anyway.) A capsule wardrobe doesn't have to mean a palette of neutral colours either; the key is that they can mix and match together – go bold if that's your style."

And what are the staple items worth investing in, according to Kim? She says, "The things worth investing in will always be the pieces we wear most often. Whether that's a pair of leather loafers, or a winter wool coat. Investing in quality usually means they will last longer and end up being what you reach for each year." So next time you find yourself adding random items to your basket, ask yourself whether your wardrobe will really benefit and stick to the timeless pieces you know you'll get value from.

PRESS THE MUTE BUTTON

Before you turn the page and tell yourself that you can't possibly mute or unfollow your friends on social media, stick with me here. There are plenty of silver linings to social media, including the ability to stay up to speed with your wider network from afar. That friend you met during your year abroad, who lives in Seattle? You can stay in touch and like their pictures to let them know you still care. But what about those close friends who constantly post their best lives and latest wins, which start to grate on you?

It can be easy to get swept up in the idea that we have to comment, follow and like everything that our network posts, regardless of how it makes us feel. But looking after your own mental wellbeing is even more important than engaging with every new update, and sometimes that may mean stepping back from social media for a minute and hitting the mute button. Muting isn't the same as blocking; it's clear to see how that might rub your friends up the wrong way and cause some serious friendship friction. Muting is a great tool to keep in your locker that can give you the headspace you need to focus on number one without your friends or family needing to know. Accepting that you need to hit mute for a bit doesn't mean you don't want to be friends with someone, or support them; it simply means that you need a break. And in the long term? That break might just have huge benefits for your real-life relationship.

PRACTISE FINANCIAL GRATITUDE

Once rooted in spiritual practices, gratitude has undergone a mainstream transformation. Science now backs up the theory that many religious and spiritual communities have long claimed: gratitude really can do a lot of good. It supports our mental wellbeing and can make us happier and feel connected to a sense of something greater than ourselves.[4]

CREATE YOUR OWN MONEY GRATITUDE PRACTICE

There are many simple ways to cultivate gratitude. Whether you want to go all-in by a keeping a special gratitude journal or simply start off with baby steps, building a regular habit of gratitude can allow you to appreciate the present and what you do have, rather than focusing on what you don't have – something that's all too easy to do.

- **List three things.** Simply think of things that you're grateful for, focusing especially on what the money you do have currently facilitates. From your morning cup of coffee to your comfy bed sheets or Spotify subscription that allows you to blast out good mood music, it's about noticing the little things we often overlook.

- **Make a daily habit of feeling grateful.** To make a daily habit of gratitude, try adding on your gratitude practice to an existing part of your routine such as brushing your teeth.

Whether you find yourself comparing your life on the regular or you've got a handle on the curse of comparison, there are endless benefits to putting in place barriers and building habits to help turn down the volume on others and zone in on your own life. There's no magic solution to remove that little voice in our heads which can pile on the pressure to perform better and achieve more, yet with the right tools in our kit then we can equip ourselves to navigate the tricky days and find contentment with what we have now, while working toward improving our future circumstances. After all, right now is all that is guaranteed – so let's make the most of it.

THE BANK OF MUM AND DAD

5

Do you remember the days at school when you dreamed of being an adult? My idea of adulthood looked like going to work in a well-fitted suit with sky-high stilettos and living in a big house with a drive and bay windows, fully funded by my reasonable but not excessive salary. A swimming pool in the garden was on the plan of action for adulthood too; after all, that's what most adult houses looked like according to the movies *Mean Girls* and *Clueless*. It all seemed a reasonable ask, as long as I did my homework and landed a good career. At least that's the dream many of us were sold growing up – that being an adult meant financial independence and standing on your own two feet. Fast forward two financial crises and a global pandemic later, it turns out that adulthood doesn't look quite like the suburban dream I was sold by the glamorous American movies and TV shows of my teenage years. As the poet and philosopher Paul Valéry puts it: "The trouble with our times is that the future is not what it used to be."

What happened to turn the teenage adulthood dream from an ambitious aim to a fantasy? The main issue is that the trajectory of adulthood today no longer resembles the path our parents and grandparents, and their predecessors before them, found themselves on. Not least because of the drastically changing economic conditions we find ourselves facing today, the time in our lives when adults are reaching traditional milestones is steadily increasing as the years go by. One significant positive change from the years gone by is that women now make up a huge part of the workforce, employed across industries and in roles that not all that long ago were solely reserved for men. Where our grandmothers stayed at home to raise families, more women today in their 20s are climbing the career ladder first and foremost. Yet we can't ignore the impact of housing policies across the last 50 years on adulthood today. The effects of decades of policy are now being felt by millions of aspiring homeowners struggling to make their home ownership dreams a reality. Plus with rapidly rising rental costs in the years post pandemic, almost one in five parents in the UK are planning for their adult children to move back to the family home due to the cost of living.[1,2] Across the Atlantic, the outlook looks scarily similar for a generation of young adults; while the majority of millennials still aspire to own a home, a combination of the deposit required, bad credit and student debt stand in the way.[3] As well as the timelines for moving out of the family home shifting to later on in life, millions of adults are now choosing to opt out of the traditional set-up altogether – sometimes solely for financial reasons.

In the UK, the track record of intergenerational progress – the idea that each generation will be better off financially than those before them – led to high hopes for the generation of adults born between 1981 and 1996, otherwise known as the oat-latte-drinking, avocado-toast-eating millennials. Similarly in the US, the idea of the American Dream has been a realistic goal, with each generation of Americans having the potential to out-earn their parents. History shows that for generations in the post-war years through to the late 20th century, the intergenerational bargain held up and each new generation did see living standards move in an upward direction. But all good things come to an end, and that end began at the turn of the century. A year immortalized in time thanks to a Robbie Williams smash hit and the Millennium Dome, when the eldest of the millennials tentatively entered adulthood. Britney Spears ruled the pop world, *American Idol* first took the TV airwaves by storm and the future looked bright for the new generation entering the workforce. But throw in a few decades of economic stagnation, low wage growth, unforeseen global crises and rampant house price inflation and those expectations are no longer holding up in the modern times. And it's not just a funny feeling that us millennials have that things aren't quite how we thought they would be during our childhood; studies suggest that generational progress in both the UK and USA is rapidly grinding to a halt.[4] The American Dream – aka the belief that upward mobility is attainable for everyone – is becoming harder to realize and it looks as though there's no imminent sign of change.[5]

As the financial pressure that modern life brings ramps up, the intergenerational contract that has been embedded in the world many of us grew up in is breaking down, and the ability to fund traditional milestones – which often have significant financial consequences – is more and more reliant on older generations. The Bank of Mum and Dad is more influential than ever before and when it comes to those traditional steps in adulthood that many of us expect to take, the gap between those with access to the Bank of Mum and Dad and those without is growing wider. Our expectations for our lives are out of line with the economic reality we face, and it's causing chaos for our mental and financial wellbeing.

What can we do to handle the financial pressure that comes with adulthood today? And how do we navigate the emotional and practical consequences of a pay-to-play system, where financial support from parents has a knock-on effect on so many aspects of our lives?

A FAMILY AFFAIR

In an increasingly expensive society, the knock-on effect of receiving a financial leg-up from a parent or caregiver might seem minimal, yet over time, the cumulative impact of seemingly small individual slices of help can snowball into vastly different outcomes. The gap between the financially privileged and less fortunate may seem narrow at birth, but as soon as you leave the hospital and get a leg up, the financial resources of your family start to influence every aspect of your life. In a truly meritocratic world, creativity, skill and innovation would be the sole factors that determined who succeeds and who struggles in any society. But although hard work and talent do have a part to play in influencing outcomes for children and adults alike, there's no denying that there is another key element that impacts your future trajectory: your financial situation. And not just your individual financial circumstances: the role of family wealth is one of the most influential factors in how easy or hard it is to reach financial stability. Of course, there will always be examples of outliers who make it without the backing of financial privilege, but it's safe to say we can't ignore the huge role that family economics plays in determining where we end up.

The domino effect of growing up financially privileged can easily be overlooked. While there's no guarantee that financial privilege will lead to a happier, more fulfilling life (that's a topic for another chapter), the fact of the matter is that money facilitates access to more opportunities from a very, very early age. Throughout Western society, scratch below the surface of many systems that look equal to all from the outside and you'll discover that with money, you can still edge the upper hand. In the UK and the US, fee-paying private schools tend to consistently produce higher exam results than government or state-funded schools. And take the state school admissions system here in the UK as a further example: the catchment area admissions process was designed to be fair and at first glance, prioritizing spaces to families living near to a school makes perfect sense. Until you realize that house prices tend to be far higher in the catchment area of high-performing state schools, pricing out families who can't afford the inflated cost of houses and creating an unofficial pay-to-play system. Look at UK grammar schools – aka the selective, non-fee paying schools which tend to perform very well academically, and which allow any student to take the entrance exam. Grammar schools offer places based on academic performance alone, giving gifted children of any background the opportunity to get into the school. Except for the fact that families with the financial means can pay tutors to spend hours and hours helping their children to prepare for the exam and boost their chances of success, effectively giving them a competitive advantage.

The school system is one of the first checkpoints in childhood where financially privileged families can give their children an advantage, and the impact of financial circumstances on your education only continues after school. University may look like an even playing field for students once you accept a place, yet the way that funding operates in the UK is a prime example of how your time at university can be wildly different based on your – or your family's – finances. Under the current university funding system, two students with identical academic records who study at exactly the same institution can end up with opposing experiences solely due to their finances. But the role that individual finances have on the university experience hasn't always been the same as it is today; as recently as in the 1960s, student loans were non-existent and university tuition was funded by local authorities.[6]

Fast forward to the 1990s and university funding shortages led to shifting government policy, slowly pushing the financial burden of higher education on to the individual student. Prior to 1998, higher education was state funded and effectively free to access across the UK for home students, with maintenance grants available to help cover living costs without any requirement to repay the money. Then in 1998, the Labour government under

Tony Blair first introduced tuition fees to address university funding issues, initially at a rate of £1,000 per year and rising to £3,000 per year in 2006. Slowly over time, the financial barriers to higher education kept creeping up, culminating in the current system that came into effect in 2012, raising tuition fees to £9,000 per year.[7] Today, students can expect to leave university with almost £30,000 of debt in tuition loans before interest is added. In the USA the cost of college is a highly debated topic with the average cost hitting almost $40,000 per year and with the ultimate cost of a bachelor's degree totalling, in some cases, an eye-watering $500,000.[8]

On this side of the Atlantic, tuition fees are only one piece of the university funding puzzle and in a similar manner to the sharp increase of tuition fees, the state funding for living costs during university years has changed from non-repayable grants to loans, which students now have to repay on an income-contingent basis. Yet still under the loan system, even the highest level of maintenance payment will rarely cover all the essential living costs for a student. The Student Money Survey found that in 2022, the average student's Maintenance Loan fell short of covering their living costs by a huge £439 every month.[9] For many students, the shortfall between government support and costs leaves no choice but to work part-time alongside their studies during further education. Even for students with minimal teaching hours, university study requires a lot of effort and the struggle to make ends meet can be an unwelcome distraction from academic work. In contrast, university students receiving financial support from family members with living expenses can focus solely on their studies and not have to worry about paying the bills. In fact, although college costs are significantly higher overall in the US than the UK, the greatest financial contribution to most students' education is parental support.

The impact of parental support goes far beyond the university years too; the UK graduate who enters the workforce without a student loan has a significantly higher take-home salary than their peers with loans to repay. Once students earn over the relevant repayment amount, 9 per cent of their salary over the threshold has to be repaid to the Student Loans Company. That's 9 per cent that students without loans have in their take-home pay packet, to save or invest for the future. To build up their house deposit or fund that business they hope to sell for millions one day. Yet it's worth noting that until you earn the threshold amount, you don't have to worry about repayments and in that respect, in the UK student loans are more akin to a graduate tax than a traditional loan (as in the USA). Although the figures may be daunting, if you're currently studying then the best course of action is to focus on your studies and maximize the experience as best as you can. Finances aside, university or college can provide a platform on which to build your career, skills and network, so try to enjoy the present and get the most out of your time at university.

Slowly and subtly but surely, financial support at each of the life stages where money plays a role can influence your ability over time to reach your next money-related goal or milestone. That's why, although equal at first glance, students with identical university degrees or with carbon-copy internship offers might find themselves in dramatically different financial situations. Being able to focus fully on your studies and participate in a month-long internship without pay rather than earn for that month-long period, or to accept an entry-level position in a sought-after industry because you can live at home nearby rent-free, can change your future. Financial privilege can have a domino effect, allowing some people to seize opportunities to set themselves up for success in the future, while other people have no choice but to funnel all of their resources toward staying financially afloat. Once the dominoes start falling in one direction or another, it becomes increasingly clear to see how the chain reaction of the financial cards we're dealt takes hold. There's one particular time when these differing situations start to come sharply into focus, though, and that's when we start talking about houses.

THE OBSESSION WITH OWNERSHIP

Millennials in Britain and the US are a generation obsessed with home ownership. In the UK, unlike our European neighbours, owning property has long been aspirational for millions of young adults. If the American Dream is the idea that with hard work alone, anyone can make it in the land of Stars and Stripes, the British dream is that owning a home is the answer. The answer to what, I have no idea – but it's crystal clear that the home ownership dream has captivated our collective imagination for decades and, oh, how the politicians have played it to their advantage as well! So it's no surprise that the topic of home ownership is one of the most highly charged issues in both the personal finance sphere and the wider economy.

To understand and unpack the home ownership obsession, it's helpful to strip back to basics and look at a small slice of human psychology. The model known as "Maslow's hierarchy of needs" provides a simple framework for understanding what motivates humans. The famous theory explores the needs of humans and breaks down our needs into a hierarchy of five core categories, with the general premise being that only once basic needs are met can people address their higher needs. According to Maslow, the most basic level of needs are physiological needs which must be met to survive, such as food, water and air. Makes sense. Then, once our physiological needs are met, humans have a need for safety. Together, physiological needs and safety needs are considered to make up basic human needs. Within the need for safety is the human need for security, and one way that we aim to fulfil our security needs in modern times is through safe, secure housing. If security in the form of a safe, reliable home is a basic need for humans and that need isn't being met by the current system, it's no surprise that people are preoccupied with finding a sure-fire way to meet that need.

Sadly, the cost of housing in major hubs in both the UK and US increasingly highlights that home ownership is becoming a privilege for the few, not the many, despite the desire of so many people to own their own home. Commentators will point to Europe when attempting to unpack the obsession with home ownership, and make the valid point that you don't need to own the bricks and mortar for a house to be your home. In fact, there are few places where the status of home ownership holds the same clout or hold over peoples' lives as it does in Britain. Yet in the context of Maslow's hierarchy and the need for security, when you take a look at the rental systems across various countries it becomes clear to see why the ownership obsession continues.

In many countries where home ownership isn't fetishized, it's notable that tenants have far stronger rights and state protection, which allows them to feel secure in their home regardless of the name on the property deed. In Germany, over 40 million tenants have the comfort and stability of knowing that most tenancies are indefinite, with evictions allowed in a very limited number of circumstances. In England, landlords can evict tenants without any justification after an initial contract period, giving tenants very little notice about the change in circumstances. There is no legislation for rent control in England, leaving the financial strain on tenants at the mercy of landlords, whereas Germany has strong restrictions on rent increases during a tenancy.[10] This heavy reliance on the good nature of a landlord in a highly unregulated UK private rental sector explains why so many aspire to have a home of their own. The lack of protection for tenants under the law and the view by many landlords that their property is simply an asset, rather than a home, only heightens the desire for many families to secure ownership of a property.

With the rental landscape in mind, it's far less surprising that the goal of taking that first step on the property ladder continues to dominate the finances of millions of young adults. Yet there are a handful of hurdles to navigate in the pursuit of property ownership. Affordability – or how much you can borrow to buy a house – has been hit hard by supercharged house price inflation, slow wage growth over recent years and the rising cost of living, leaving many hopeful future homeowners scratching their heads over how to make the maths add up. The circumstances for aspiring homeowners in North America are alike, too; a Forbes deep dive found that seven in ten millennials living in big cities or their suburbs found their living situation hard or extremely hard to afford.[11] And with older generations quick to point out that millennials spend too much money on holidays and avocado toast, you might be asking yourself whether you've missed a memo on how to fund a house purchase.

It's safe to say that whichever way you cut the data, housing is significantly more expensive now than just a few decades ago, even when adjusted for inflation. For example, in the mid-1990s, UK house prices stood at around four times average earnings, yet 30 years later they are more than eight times the average salary, highlighting how affordability has dramatically declined for young people trying to buy their first home.[12] In the US, house prices have soared by 118 per cent since 1965, during which time average income has only increased by 15 per cent (all inflation-adjusted figures).[13] Even with the huge rise in house prices, which has long outpaced earnings increases, banks are reluctant to lend borrowers more than around five times their salary to fund a home purchase, so average earners who once could've secured a home without trouble will now struggle to find affordable housing in many areas of the country with simply their own financial means. Which is why a Rightmove- and Zillow-addicted generation of aspiring property owners can find themselves staring at the gap between their friends' entry level job and the property they live in and wind up with one conclusion: the Bank of Mum and Dad.

WHAT 49 PER CENT OF FIRST-TIME BUYERS AREN'T TELLING YOU

In a fragile financial sector following the 2023 collapse of US financial institution Silicon Valley Bank, and with the long-term effects of an inflation-fuelled cost-of-living crisis not yet fully known, there's one lender booming to new heights year on year: the Bank of Mum and Dad. Although not quite an official financial institution, the Bank of Mum and Dad contributes an estimated 26 per cent of funds to the UK housing market, placing parents as effectively the ninth biggest lender in the country.[14] With house prices out of reach for so many working adults, reliance on financial help from parents shows no sign of slowing down. The Institute of Fiscal Studies found that around £17bn is now gifted or loaned by parents to their adult children each year, predominantly to help with property purchases or marriage and usually occurring when children are in their late 20s or early 30s.[15]

The prospect of a healthy pile of cash from the Bank of Mum and Dad can, for many, make the seemingly impossible house purchase possible. The financial situation that a number of baby boomers – now in their 60s and 70s – have found themselves in has allowed them the capital to help their families onto the property ladder. For many of the older generation, the stark contrast of the housing market faced by their hard-working children is clear and some parents are keen to do what they can to help secure their children financially for the future.

But receiving financial support isn't always straightforward emotionally, particularly for adult children who are independent and want to stand on their own two feet. For some recipients of help funding a property purchase, there's an unease that comes hand in hand with the gratitude. Catherine, 36, recently bought a flat with the help of her parents. After a break-up with a previous partner, the prospect of owning a place in London where she was born and raised seemed out of reach, despite working extremely hard to increase her salary. Her parents benefited from huge house price inflation and, on selling the family home, had the cash available to help Catherine with footing most of the deposit for her flat.

Catherine explained her mixed emotions about the situation she finds herself in: "I'm intensely grateful for the help, but I also feel ashamed. I've worked very hard all my life, not only to get top grades and a degree from a leading university, but also in paid work from the week after my 16th birthday. But it's not been enough." And what about the attitudes of society toward young people and their inability to get on the property ladder? She says, "There's a cultural narrative that young people spend too much and while I've never lived beyond my means or bought any kind of luxury or designer item, I have been on a few holidays and eaten out sometimes. I also chose to work in public service and have a positive impact, so it feels like the fault is mine." Catherine is by no means alone, and although the media may have painted millennials and Gen Z as avocado-obsessed, brunch-loving spenders, the statistics show in black and white that the landscape has shifted immeasurably for aspiring homeowners.

The gift of hefty financial help doesn't always come baggage-free, either. Although her parents bought Lucy (not her real name) and her sister a flat in London worth around £2m during her university studies, family relations have become difficult around the issue. When Lucy decided to pursue a career path less traditional than her sister, the treatment of the sisters became notably different and after Lucy moved out of the flat for a period of time, her sister rented out her room to a friend. Although Lucy planned to return, her parents sided with her older sister and haven't allowed Lucy to move back into the flat, giving her no say over who lives there or how much rent they pay. I asked Lucy how she feels about the situation currently and she told me, "Having [money gifted] definitely can put a strain on family relationships but having something to your name, an asset that is valuable and always there if something happens, is definitely something that can only help in the future. But it is never as easy as it looks and just because a person has help, it doesn't mean that everything came easy or was handed over or that family relationships are solid and amazing. There's always something you don't know about the situation."

Even in family settings where parental help isn't available in hard cash, the time and skills dedicated to helping out family members can have a huge indirect financial benefit to your bank balance. We can be quick to overlook the ways that other forms of family help can boost our finances, yet the impact on your bank balance of childcare support from parents or living at the family home for years can be life-changing. Emily was one of three and although her parents didn't have the money to gift toward her first home, they helped in other significant ways. She explains, "My parents have always given time and they have my little boy while we work on the house. We've also been super lucky that my partner's dad is a builder and so when we get quotes we ask his advice as to whether it's a good quote or not. Again, he doesn't have the ability to support with finances, but he has helped with the build and plastering."

One thing that seems clear is that feelings are divided about the role and reliance on the Bank of Mum and Dad. For many beneficiaries of help, there are conflicting feelings about the economic situation we find ourselves in, both among those with and those without hefty family financial support. Research from the Institute for Fiscal Studies shows that wealth transfers only serve to increase inequality between young adults, with over half of the £17bn value of transfers given by the wealthiest fifth of adults – almost exclusively homeowners and disproportionately living in London and the South East.[16]

The natural question that the data leads to is how on earth should we navigate generational wealth if and when we're one day in the driving seat of decision-making ourselves? The challenge of how to balance the desire not to further fuel an inherently unequal system, combined with the knowledge that if you don't play the game, your future children or family might get left behind, is something many adults will be grappling with for years to come.

WHAT ASPIRING HOMEOWNERS NEED TO KNOW

In the absence of a crystal ball revealing the future of the housing market, here are a handful of thoughts to keep in mind if you are finding it tricky to escape the feeling that the financial cards are stacked against you. Firstly, take a moment to figure out what your own financial goals truly are, rather than what you think they should be. Home ownership has long been on the traditional list of goals, yet the structure of our working lives is shifting and, increasingly, people are starting to question whether the house and 2.4 children is for them.

If you do decide that home ownership is a goal you want to pursue, remember that you're not in a race and there really is no rush to hit any "milestones", financial or otherwise. While there are a number of pros to owning your property, it's not the right move for everyone and if flexibility to travel frequently or the potential to move abroad is on your radar, putting down roots in one place with a chunky financial commitment might not be the best decision for you. When you're laser-focused on reaching a goal, it's easy to zone in on the downsides to renting or living with parents, so instead challenge yourself to shift your perspective. Remember that the freedom of renting and lack of responsibility are real, tangible benefits to *not* being a homeowner.

Practically speaking, there are two main ingredients to consider with a property purchase: the deposit and the mortgage. Unless you have a locker room full of cash to purchase a property in full, you'll need to borrow money from a lender in the form of a mortgage. Most lenders require borrowers to provide a cash deposit in order to borrow money, so that the risk of property price fluctuations is spread between the homeowner and lender. How much you can borrow will vary between lenders and largely depend on your income, as well as your affordability – aka what lenders believe you can comfortably repay. As a ballpark estimate, most lenders will allow you to borrow between four and five times your salary, although your spending will be taken into account before a mortgage offer is put on the table. If you plan to purchase a home with a partner, you can borrow based on both incomes rather than just one. Keep in mind that if you do split up, however, one of you will have to buy the other partner out of the property (which can be expensive) or you'll need to sell your home to distribute any value in the house.

Mortgage aside, the main hurdle for many aspiring homeowners is the deposit. As house prices have rocketed over recent decades, the amount of cash needed to put down a deposit – which is typically between 10 to 20 per cent of the property value – has simultaneously increased. With the cost of living sky-high over the last few years and rental prices going in one direction, it's no surprise that people are struggling to save month on month to get closer to their property goals. Although it may feel hard at times, there are ways to make the process of saving for a deposit easier. Focus your attention on streamlining your budget and getting clear on how much you have coming in and going out of your account each month. Saving for a large sum of money such as a deposit is a long game, so give yourself the best chance of success by setting up a direct deposit into your savings account when you get paid. By paying yourself first, your savings become non-negotiable and you don't rely on having money left over by payday to add to your savings pot.

Take a look at the government schemes available to help first-time buyers. For UK residents between the age of 18 and 40, a Lifetime ISA (LISA) could give you a 25 per cent boost on your home savings if you meet the eligibility criteria.[17] In 2021, the UK government also introduced a mortgage guarantee scheme to help buyers secure mortgages with a 5 per cent deposit.[18] In the US, first-time home buyer programmes exist to help buyers by offering loans with reduced mortgage rates, along with 100 per cent backed mortgage options to increase access to borrowing.[19] Even if you choose to use a scheme, aiming for a higher deposit can give you access to more competitive interest rates; however, the chance to purchase a home with a lower deposit is a welcome option for lots of households. Whether your timeline to become a homeowner is six months or six years, work out how much you can set aside each month to get closer to your total target and remember not to compare your timeline to anyone else: we're all on our own unique paths in this life and there is no race to run.

DEALING WITH FAMILY FINANCES

We all know that whether you love them or loathe them, family relationships can be the source of the highest highs and the greatest challenges. Handling financial matters with your relatives can be difficult for a whole host of reasons. The unique relationship we each have with our finances ties closely to the lessons we learned – consciously or not – about money from our caregivers at a young age, and the impact of money on family dynamics can't be underestimated. The people we care about the most can be the hardest to set boundaries with, especially with topics as highly charged as money. Yet there are many situations where setting boundaries around money is critical, not only for the long-term health of the relationship but for your own financial wellbeing too. When Rose's brother decided to set up a business, for example, he asked her for money despite not really needing the financial help, which then put a strain on Rose's relationship with her own partner. She explains, "I tried to help my family all the time when they didn't really need my help! But the guilt kicks in a lot. My partner had to put strict boundaries in place for both of us with my family in terms of money."

It's clear that it's all well and good sitting here saying that financial boundaries are important, but it can be extremely tough emotionally and practically to put them in place. To understand how you can go about setting boundaries to protect your own financial health, I spoke to an expert in the field. Dr Tari Mack, a clinical psychologist with over 20 years of experience, helps clients to navigate family dynamics. When I asked Dr Mack how someone might deal with the situation where a close family member repeatedly asks for financial help, she told me, "Figure out what the truth is – perhaps it's that you're not comfortable continuing to give them money – and then find a kind way to say it. It doesn't mean that they're going to hear it and not be upset. You can't control that, but you want to be two things: kind and honest." Dr Mack believes that in this situation, it's highly likely there's a pattern of behaviour that goes beyond money. This behaviour can encompass beliefs you hold about your role in the family and, sometimes, your perspective about whether you feel as though your personal needs matter in comparison to others in your family. 'If you find yourself in this situation, begin exploring your beliefs," she advises. "Ask yourself: what role do you play in the family dynamic? Why have you had that role? How is it working for you? It is possible to change that role," she notes. Difficult as it may be, there might be times when you have to prioritize your own financial wellbeing over helping someone else, but even if you cannot help out with cash, think about whether you can provide support in other ways, such as signposting organizations to help with money issues or debt charities.

If you are in a position to be able to help out financially, consider how to approach a loan and what the possible outcomes of that scenario might be. If there's a chance that the money may never be repaid, be confident that you can afford the loan before you go ahead. Formalizing the loan with a contract can be a wise idea, too, so that all parties involved have clear expectations of how much money is being loaned, for how long and on what terms. That way, you stand the best chance of avoiding misunderstandings and harming the relationship.

HOW TO LOOK AFTER YOUR FAMILY AFFAIRS

There are three topics of conversation that modern society typically loves to avoid talking about in the open: sex, money and death. Right now, we're about to dive head-first into two of the three: death and money. In a picture-perfect world I'd be able to confidently reassure you that family bonds are far stronger than money. But we all know that I'd be lying, as the truth is that money has been a major cause of family conflicts for all of time, and yet millions of families still opt to avoid the topic. Not any longer.

Granted, spending your Sunday roast family time talking about death might not be at the top of your dream weekend list. But joking aside, having a frank discussion about financial plans for later life with your family – in particular your parents or close family – is a worthwhile conversation, and it can save the entire family from a whole load of unwanted stress down the line. Avoiding the topic of death doesn't make it less likely to happen and you simply kick the can down the road until a later date, leaving the door open to a situation where you have to deal head-on with all the things you didn't discuss earlier, at a time when you may be grieving. The reality is that whether it's now or in the distant future, family deaths will happen and being prepared with the paperwork can help reduce the to-do list at a traumatic time. So whether you have a little or a lot, there are some key steps to take in order to ensure a person's wishes are fulfilled if they fall ill or when they pass away. Here is a rundown of the need-to-know documents to keep your and your family's affairs in order.

A WILL
Officially known as a last will and testament, a will is a legal document that outlines your wishes on how you want to distribute your assets. This can include anything and everything you own, including property, cash and jewellery. If you don't leave a will, which is known as dying intestate, the decision about

who will inherit your assets will be determined by the law and you can leave family members in a very difficult financial position.

Having a will is a wise idea at any stage of life, so you can rest easy, knowing that your wishes will be fulfilled if anything happens to you. Even if a will seems low down your priority to-do list, there are certain circumstances where a will is an absolute essential to protect your family and make sure that your assets end up with the intended beneficiaries. Imagine this scenario: you've separated from a spouse and happily live with a new partner, but you haven't yet legally divorced. Without a will, if you pass away suddenly then your estranged spouse will inherit your assets, potentially leaving your new partner homeless. Writing a will gives you control over what happens when you're no longer here and the ability to leave things exactly the way you wish. Whether you want to donate all your belongings to charity, have a specifically themed send-off or gift a particular piece of jewellery to a person you have in mind, writing a will is an empowering and positive act, rather than something with the morbid association it often seems to carry. Plus it's an act of care to your family and friends to help guide them at a difficult time.

You can write a will without the help of a solicitor, although it's worth considering professional help if the will is complicated in any way. If you share property with someone that isn't a spouse, you have a complicated relationship with your family or you have specific unusual wishes for your estate, working with a lawyer can help you to avoid mistakes which could invalidate your will. If you do wish to write your own will but need a guide, there are plenty of low-cost services to help such as Make A Will Online and FreeWill.

POWER OF ATTORNEY

Power of attorney is a legal way to ensure that financial decisions, along with medical decisions, can be made by someone you trust if you're no longer able to make decisions yourself. Your parents may wish to appoint you as a power of attorney so that you're able to make decisions about their property and finances in the event that they are no longer able to, whether for a short period of time or, more often, as a result of illness or old age. Having a valid power of attorney gives everyone involved the knowledge that everyday tasks such as paying bills are under control.

To make a lasting power of attorney, the individual making the appointment of an attorney must complete the relevant forms either online or in paper form. In the UK, for the power of attorney to be valid, it must be registered with the Office of the Public Guardian (OPG), which can take up to 20 weeks, so keep in mind that it isn't a quick process. For US citizens, in most states you will have to have the POA witnessed by a notary, so be sure to look up the requirements in your specific state. The type of power of attorney will determine in what circumstances you can make decisions on behalf of the person appointing you.

৪৯

While time will tell how the role of the Bank of Mum and Dad will continue to evolve, it undoubtedly plays a huge part in the opportunities, choices and decisions so many of us make with money. Whether you've received financial help from your family or not, understanding the scale of parental support can help make sense of how people navigate this ever-expensive world we live in.

Hopefully by now, you've got a clearer idea of both the importance of starting sometimes tricky conversations with your nearest and dearest, as well as the practical side of things. The idea of paperwork and administration centred on illness and death might seem gloomy, but when the time comes then you can save yourself and your family from additional stress at a difficult time. Some families choose to write funeral wishes in advance too, which can ensure that every person has the chance to have the send-off they hope for. So why not flip your perspective on family affairs and view this as an opportunity to plan your final party as you'd like. Now who doesn't want to have a say in that?

YOU'RE INVITED

6

Growing up in the 2000s under the heavy influence of MTV's *My Super Sweet Sixteen*, from long before I entered the teenage years myself, I had the idea planted in my mind early on that at some point in the future, I'd have my red carpet moment. Fast forward into adulthood and from hen parties to week-long weddings, "dirty thirty" celebrations to gender reveal events, every landmark moment is now an opportunity to get together, make memories . . . and spend some hard-earned cash. That's not to say that the only way to mark these special occasions is to throw a supersized expensive party, but in the age of social media – where our phones are never far from our hands and we document daily snippets of our lives online – it's become increasingly normal for milestones to be marked in Instagram-worthy style.

Over the last few decades, slowly but surely these milestone events are happening at a later stage in our lives. With less traditional life stages being the norm, along with the increased cost of housing and shifting financial priorities, traditional occasions that once were celebrated over a five- or ten-year period are being condensed into a small number of years, often when we are in our late 20s and early 30s. In the 1970s, the average age in the UK for a first-time marriage was 22 for women and 25 for men, whereas today the numbers stand almost a decade later – at 31 and 33 respectively.[1] According to *Brides* magazine, these figures are 28.6 and 30.4 in the USA, signalling an increase of a decade in the last century.[2] The fact that these significant – and expensive – events are happening later can be a blessing on the one hand, as this allows more time for everyone to establish their careers and boost earnings before the costs of celebrations kick in. But at the same time, the compressed timelines can ramp up the financial squeeze in the years when many people are focused on achieving financial goals of their own. Traditional milestones in life – which happened in the early to mid-20s a few decades ago, such as buying a first home – are taking longer to reach. The rapid rise of house prices has shifted the age of first-time homeowners well into the 30s, with the average first-time buyer now aged 33 across the UK.[3]

The knock-on effect of these landmark events occurring later on in our lives means that it's not unusual to hit your late 20s and find your annual leave allowance for the next three or four years – and your entire holiday budget – spoken for by your social calendar. With stag and hen parties, weekend-long weddings, birthday parties or baby showers, the cost of celebrations just seems to keep on going up and up.

LAST FLING BEFORE THE RING

One time during my legal training contract, my supervisor came into the office, excited for her weekend ahead. At this point, I already knew that her glamorous wedding was on the horizon; however, one topic we'd not discussed was the hen party. Expecting the response to be something along the lines of a bougie spa weekend or trip to Soho Farmhouse, my eyes were opened to a new world when she announced she was off to Dubai for her hen party – not for her honeymoon, but the pre-wedding celebration with a group of her closest friends. Granted, she was a partner at a law firm, but until that moment I'd thought long-haul travel for stag and hen dos was something reserved for celebrities, or overexcited grooms on *Don't Tell The Bride* (which I admittedly spent far too many hours watching to figure out exactly what I didn't want any future wedding I might have to look like). Little did I know quite what lay in store when it came to the reality of celebrating milestones in the modern world.

My experience of hen parties started off early on, when the first of my close friends became engaged at a time when most of us had barely woken up from last night's hangover. With a four-year-long degree, I was still in my early 20s and finishing my studies when I realized that not only was a wedding on the horizon, but the prospect of my first hen party. On the basis that a significant number of students and recent graduates would be attending, the organizers prioritized how to have the best time for the bride on a budget. But fast forward a few years, more stable careers and slightly healthier bank balances and suddenly the expectations for stags, hens and celebrations became supercharged – along with the cost of the events to go with them.

I mentioned earlier how the saying goes that friends are the family you choose for yourself, and there's nothing that many of us love more than coming together to celebrate the happiness of our favourite people. Without doubt, I'm an old-school romantic at heart, so I'm the first to jump at any opportunity to recognize love and cheer for it. It seems that I'm not alone; in the UK, the size of hen parties is on the rise, with an average of 15 guests joining the party in 2023. While 67 per cent of hens stay in the country, 33 per cent head abroad.[4] Yet even in the UK, the cost of attending a hen party can be several hundred pounds and when you start to add up the number of hens in a year the financial pressure can start to mount up.

With so many factors influencing the cost of a hen do and a lack of general consensus about what the norms look like for these occasions, I asked my online community about their experiences. From a single activity day in the local area through to week-long luxury trips abroad, it soon became clear that there is no one-size-fits-all hen party experience. Alongside the event itself, the range of costs for attending a party quickly spanned from under £100 to £3,000 at the highest end. In response to the question of what people felt to be a reasonable amount to spend, the figure that surfaced landed predominantly in the £200 to £300 range for a weekend. That being said, it was by no means unanimous and most guests typically expect hen dos abroad to be more expensive, even though some UK destinations come close these days.

Digging into the cost of a hen party, one theme that cropped up time and time again was the pressure to attend extravagant events, especially among bridesmaids and close friends of the bride. Recent destination hen parties spanned far and wide, including Ibiza, Marbella, Mykonos, Marrakech and the Middle East, to name a few – with one bridesmaid spending £3,000 on a hen party to Dubai as well as with a UK-based celebration for the same bride. As a bridesmaid, Milly felt as though she couldn't say no to the bride's idea to go to Dubai, leaving her feeling the pressure to find the money to attend. Another bridesmaid, Sarah, is in the midst of planning a hen party but dealing with high expectations from the bride. She says, "The couple are doing a massive abroad wedding and the bride wanted to do an abroad hen. But I asked the hens how much they wanted to spend and it's not that much, as they have to fly and get accommodation for the wedding. I'm stuck between a rock and a hard place of the bride being demanding, wanting a luxury party weekend, and the reality of the budget." Another hen party guest spent £1,000 on a hen party in Ibiza: "It was a five-day trip, including beach clubs and club nights. The Maid of Honour only shared the plan with the group once we'd all agreed to go."

After speaking to hundreds of women about attending hen parties, I'm convinced that the idea of a send-off with your best friends can make for a brilliant occasion. Yet among the women that I spoke to, there seemed to be a commonly shared sense of sadness that the expectations of a hen party have shifted with the rise of social media and the perceived need to create a picture-perfect extravagant event. So brides and future brides, a few words of wisdom: your nearest and dearest want to celebrate you, but sometimes the expectations of hen parties simply cost too much money. For many, it just isn't possible to find hundreds of pounds for a night or weekend away (especially when you may have multiple hen dos to attend within a matter of months). It doesn't mean they love you any less. Perhaps, instead of heading straight to Skyscanner and dreaming about bringing your luxury hen party ideas to life, think about what matters to you the most. Is your priority the experience, or the people you're spending time with? Ultimately, you can have the most incredible time with the people you love and feel special without spending a fortune, so get crystal clear on what matters to you most and build your hen party experience around that. When you look back in years to come, the laughter will be the number one thing you remember. Trust me on that.

HOW NOT TO BE A BRIDEZILLA

If you are a bride-to-be, here are some simple questions to help you plan your hen do:

- Who would you like to attend your hen party? Write down a list of your invitees to give yourself an idea of the size of the party.

- Looking at your list, are there any practical considerations for your guests? Think about how the location, responsibilities or financial constraints may be a factor.

- Are there any activities that are absolute musts, or a no-go for your dream hen do?

- What budget do you consider reasonable to spend on attending a hen party? Is there a number or a range that comes to mind?

- Finally, which is more important to you: having all your guests be able to attend, or having an extravagant hen party?

THE EXPENSE OF EVENTS

Once the elation of a wedding announcement settles and the date is duly saved in the diary, the practicalities start to set in and if you are a guest, there will be plenty of plans – and costs – to think about. Even with the most simple expenses of attending a wedding, you can soon find yourself spending hundreds on travelling to and from the wedding venue and resting your dancing feet at the end of the night. And that's before we even touch on the topic of destination weddings.

The destination wedding market is booming, with one in four UK couples now opting to tie the knot abroad and similarly, 25 per cent of all US couples choosing destination weddings.[5] Unsurprisingly, the weather is the main reason given by Brits for choosing a destination wedding, with couples keen to escape the unpredictable seasons of the UK in favour of sunnier climates. Natalie got married in the south of France, choosing an idyllic chateau venue in the Languedoc region. "We always said we'd like a destination wedding for a few different reasons," she told me. "We wanted a smaller wedding, and both felt that getting married abroad helped with limiting the guest list." Did the expense of attending a destination wedding for guests come up during the wedding planning, I asked. She replied, "We did consider the cost of attending the wedding for guests – although it was 2015 and the exchange rate was more appealing. When we decided on our venue 18 months prior to our wedding, we sent out save the dates with information of where to stay and that meant that people could plan in advance. It also meant our guests could book their flights a year in advance to help spread the cost." Giving plenty of notice can be a huge help for guests when it comes to budgeting and annual leave planning, so do keep in mind the travel requirements when you start to think about setting a date.

A notable shift in the post-pandemic wedding world seems to be that there is no longer a standard way to do weddings. Whether you want a micro-wedding or supersize affair, the options for tying the knot are ever increasing and more than ever, creating a day that ticks your boxes has replaced the standard run of order. Times are a-changing, and the once traditional aspects of a wedding are evolving with the world we now live in. In fact, plenty of couples are opting to skip a wedding altogether, comfortable with their commitment without the need for a specific day to define their relationship status. Equally, the restrictions of 2020/21 saw the emergence of the micro-wedding, which has endured in popularity, with couples choosing to simplify their day and spare the expense of a bells-and-whistles wedding by heading to the registry office and hosting a small, intimate dinner for their closest friends and family. Not only are there more options than ever before when it comes to commitment within a couple, but with the cost of living continually on the rise then a small affair can save thousands.

For anyone attending a traditional-style wedding, one customary expense that wedding guests have long had to consider is the wedding registry, aka gift list, traditionally pinned as a way to help set up new couples at the start of their married lives together. When marriage took place long before property purchases, a gift of pristine Le Creuset pans or a Wedgwood vase was a perfect way to mark the milestone of marriage for newly hitched couples. Yet times have changed and priorities have shifted, so many couples have chosen to prioritize getting on the property ladder and pressed pause on wedding plans. As a result, the need for couples to be kitted out with a house full of cutlery sets and wine glasses has diminished and, instead, new-style guest lists are popping up. From each guest gifting their favourite book, to charity donations for a meaningful cause, these new-style registries have opened up ways for guests to wish couples well without adding lots of extra costs to the occasion.

BUILDING A WEDDING BUDGET

As a girl who had a Pinterest wedding board from her early 20s before any potential suitor surfaced, getting married had long been on my adulting wish list. Yet increasingly, the perception of marriage is shifting and, for many couples, getting married is neither a priority nor something they feel strongly about one way or the other. With the traditional wedding less popular, it's now becoming more and more common for couples to get married in a way that feels authentic and unique. From having a friend act as a celebrant to hosting a festival-style event with no formalities, there's really no one way to plan a wedding today. Yet the single thing that still stands is that most brides and grooms hope for their wedding day to be a once-in-a-lifetime experience, where you come together to celebrate love with your favourite people in the world. Every part of the event – from the music to the venue to the guest list – is your chance to design the day that you want to remember for years to come.

There's no hiding from the fact that paying for a wedding can be quite an undertaking and in the absence of a trust fund the size of Shiv Roy's in *Succession*, building your wedding budget might just be your biggest financial challenge to date. With the average cost of a wedding now standing at £18,400 in the UK and $30,000 in the US, figuring out exactly how to factor in every aspect of your dream day without breaking the bank can be a daunting task.[6] To give yourself the best shot at sticking to a budget, set aside time to sit down early on in your engagement and go through the financial planning process. By setting a realistic budget at the start of the process, you can avoid setting your heart on specifics until you have a clear idea of the full financial picture.

Early on in your engagement, make a special occasion out of the wedding admin and work through all of the elements of your big day that you need to consider, from the big decisions such as the venue, through to the finer details like the floral arrangements. Together, think about what matters most to you as a couple when you picture your big day, then organize the list in order of your priorities. Once you have clarity on where you want to focus your budget, you have your north star to return to when the time inevitably comes to make tough decisions about spending and saving along the path to the altar.

Asking for contributions toward your wedding can be tricky, and there's no denying that conversations about funding a wedding aren't exactly the most romantic part of the occasion.

Regardless of romance, if you plan to speak to your family about contributing financially to your wedding, then the sooner you raise the topic, the better informed you'll be about your financial situation. Raising the question of gifting money with parents can feel strange, particularly if you haven't had a conversation of this nature with them before. Instead of diving straight in with a request over dinner, research costs before you sit down to ask about contributions, so you have an idea of what the wedding costs may total. Explain your hopes and plans for the wedding to your parents, so that they have an understanding of what you're imagining. Having a clear figure as to how much you and your partner plan to spend can also help, as it can show your commitment to the event and that you have thought through the finances seriously.

However, many families aren't in a position to fund a significant chunk of a wedding, so don't feel as though you're the odd one out if you find yourself in this situation, too. Back in the olden days, weddings signified the handing over of a woman's ownership from her father to her new husband and tradition dictated that the father of the bride funded the wedding as part of the dowry (the payment made by the bride's family to her husband). Thankfully, times have changed; women are no longer viewed as the property of men and when it comes to paying for a wedding, there really isn't an approach set in stone. It's now increasingly common for couples to fund their own wedding in full, although many families still contribute in one way or another to the special occasion.

Once you settle into full-blown decision-making mode, think about how your proposed plans might impact your bank balance, as well as how much guests will need to spend to attend your special day. A number of the major planning decisions you make as a bride and groom will place the financial burden either on you, as the hosts, or shift the cost onto your guests. One popular money-saving tip for couples is to choose a weekday to get married, rather than paying for weekend venue hire, which can be hugely more expensive. While many couples opt for this approach to secure their ideal venue and stick to a budget, the financial impact instead simply shifts to the guests, who are required to take annual leave in order to attend. Guests can often feel put in a tricky position, particularly if they have a limited amount of holiday to take but want to celebrate with their friends and family. All that is to say there isn't a right or wrong approach and what works for you may not work for another couple, but where you can, flip the script and think about the potential financial impact of your plans on everyone involved.

CREATIVE WAYS TO SAVE ON YOUR BIG DAY

Planning a wedding on a budget can be the perfect opportunity to think creatively and make your wedding a uniquely personal event – memorable for all the right reasons!

Swap paper for digital invites

Beautiful though wedding stationary may be, the cost of it can quickly add up and before you know it, "save the dates", invitations and "on the day" stationary can exceed triple digits. Even if you still plan to have printed orders of service and table menus on the big day, skip the stationery in the run-up in favour of a wedding website. Options such as With Joy and Hitched give you the creative freedom to set up a wedding site for free which will allow you to monitor RSVPs, communicate with guests and add directions if you wish. The best part? Many of the website services are free of charge.

Shop second-hand

Not all that long ago, brides would have shuddered at the mere mention of shopping second-hand for a wedding dress. Yet as a result of rising awareness of sustainability and the environment in the world of fashion, the wedding dress industry has caught up and the trend of second-hand dresses and bridal rental is booming. Rather than spending a small fortune on a one-wear outfit, it's now easier than ever to find an amazing outfit at a fraction of the price you pay for made-to-measure bridal gowns. Good for the purse, good for the planet. Alternatively, how about choosing a beautiful dress that you can use again? There's no rule that requires your dress to be white and bridal, so why not invest in an outfit you can tweak and reuse for years to come.

Keep the bridal party small

Having all of your best friends as bridesmaids can start off as a sweet gesture but quickly turn into a logistical nightmare and put a huge amount of pressure on your budget. For brides planning to pay for dresses, hair and makeup, the cost of preparing each bridesmaid for the day can be several hundred dollars or pounds – never mind negotiating dresses that suit every body shape. Instead, stick to a couple of your closest friends and put the money you save toward the bar tab for everyone to enjoy.

Go handmade

If your plan is to transform your wedding Pinterest board into a reality, think creatively about how you can bridge any gaps in your budget. Use your own crafts skills to bring homemade touches to the day, or harness the power of friends and family to bring your dream wedding decor to life. Perhaps bring your bridesmaids together to create table decorations from scratch, or bake a whole host of cupcakes to build a dessert table instead of a traditional wedding cake. There are so many innovative ways to save money and bring an added homemade touch to your special day, whatever your wedding budget.

Choose buffet style

The catering is one of the most expensive elements of a wedding and a three-course meal with canapes can quickly eat up thousands from your budget. Depending on the style of wedding you choose, a buffet menu can provide a far more cost-effective option to feed your guests delicious food without spending a small fortune. In particular for self-catered venues, explore sharing plate options and you can find yourself saving a serious amount of money to allocate elsewhere.

A GUIDE FOR BRIDESMAIDS

The title of Maid of Honour is a privilege and often a nod to your importance to the bride, yet alongside the appreciation it shows, there's a fair amount of responsibility that comes with the role too. From supporting the bride in the weeks and months ahead of the big day, to executing the hen party smoothly, there's a lot to think about when you're one of the bridesmaids. Balancing the bride's expectations with those of all the guests and a budget can be challenging, especially when there are multiple opinions in the room. One way to make the planning process simpler? Ask the bride what is most important to her about the occasion.

As part of the preparations for her sister's upcoming wedding, Amy found herself in the midst of planning a weekend-long hen party for 15 people. The bridesmaids agreed to stick to a budget of £300 per person; however, the majority of that budget went on the accommodation. Amy explained how the bridesmaids allocated the budget across the weekend: "The bride said she didn't want activities, so we chose to spend the money on a lovely house and then we'll do home-based activities to keep people entertained." Had sticking to the budget been straightforward, and have all the bridesmaids been on the same page with plans? I asked, to which Amy replied, "We've definitely butted up against a bit of expectation versus reality, particularly with the cost of staycations going through the roof. Dinner is proving a bit of a sticking point in terms of price, as the other hens wanted a private chef, which is way out of budget." If you do find yourself in charge of organizing a hen party, you can use your position of power positively, particularly when it comes to the event budget. To help navigate the tricky topic of money on a hen, I've put together a how-to guide for future bridesmaids and Maids of Honour.

HOW TO HANDLE THE FINANCES OF A HEN PARTY

Communication is key. Talk openly with both the bride and the other hens about the plans you have in mind and, crucially, give the hens an idea about the expected budget for the activities as soon as you can. Even if you want to keep the details a surprise for the bride, speak to them about their initial ideas about the location of the hen party and what they think is a reasonable budget. If you're dealing with a demanding bride, remind them of the main purpose of the event, which is spending time with their nearest and dearest.

Agree a budget up front

Ideally, speak to the hens about costs before you decide on a concrete plan for the hen party, so you can gather feedback and make sure the plan is as inclusive as possible price-wise. Although it might require some delicate conversations, especially if you have a bride with high expectations, try to find an option that gives the bride a special day at the same time as not putting too much financial pressure on attendees. Be clear about what is or isn't included in the budget, too, so that no unexpected financial surprises appear at the end of the event.

Focus your attention

Once you have agreed a budget, focus your attention on the areas where you want to prioritize spending and, in turn, where you can save money. For each unique bride this can look different, and the overall style or theme of the hen party will influence the spending decisions as well. Whether you decide to focus on a weekend in the countryside or a city trip packed with activities, spend the majority of your budget on the parts of the hen do that will most elevate the overall experience for the bride.

Simplicity wins

If you have a limited budget for a hen weekend away, there are lots of creative ways to have a great time without spending a fortune. Switch out expensive restaurants or private dining and team up to cook a feast together for a fraction of the cost. Instead of hiring outside entertainment for the evening, go old-school with films and popcorn or host a games night. Ask every guest to bring along their favourite game. You can end up with a game for everyone, from Twister to Cards Against Humanity, and spend the evening in hysterics without any extra cost.

Be financially flexible

Even with the best will in the world, organizing a truly memorable hen party rarely comes for free. For the most part, hen parties bring together a mixed group of people from a wide cross section of the bride's life, meaning that every attendee is likely to have different financial means. What each individual can comfortably spend on the event will vary, so keep in mind that what you consider to be reasonable may be expensive for others. If at all possible, offering a payment plan can be helpful for more costly hen parties, although do make sure not to pressurize guests to attend if they decide to decline the party due to the costs or otherwise.

STAYING FINANCIALLY AFLOAT IN CELEBRATION SEASON

Setting your own boundaries with money ahead of an expensive season of celebrations is essential for your own financial wellbeing. It may not always come naturally, but putting in place firm boundaries can help you determine what you can commit to financially without compromising your long-term financial health. Boundaries often feel tough to enforce because no one wants to feel like the boring one, and the fear of missing out is real, but the impact of constantly allowing your boundaries to be pushed can land you in hot water financially. Not everyone will readily accept your boundaries, so be prepared for a little pushback and have responses to hand to use if needed. Stock answers such as "I'd love to be there; however, I've already allocated all of my budget this month" or "Thank you for the invitation! It'd be great to catch up but I'm currently saving for a trip, so could we have coffee instead?" can help you navigate last-minute invitations, so that when those headline invitations do come around, you've got the funds to commit to the events that matter.

As well as setting your own boundaries, get practical and start to save early to help your bank balance stay in the black once your calendar starts to fill up with social events. Before you know it, a couple of busy weekends can quickly become long weekends abroad and exotic hen parties. If you're watching diary invitations come in thick and fast and wondering how on earth to manage the financial demands, here are some simple ways you can stay on top of your spending during a busy social season.

SET UP A CELEBRATION SINKING FUND

First things first, set up a celebration sinking fund to ring-fence the cash you know you'll eventually need to spend when the chief bridesmaid comes calling. Here's how a sinking fund works: each month, you set aside a slice of your salary for a specific purpose and over time, you build up the pot of money, rather than having to face a big expense in one go. When you know you've got costs coming up, sinking funds will take the sting out of paying up and help you stay afloat with your budget as well. Even if you don't yet have an exact figure for the cost of an event, most party organizers will have a target spend in mind, so ask them for an estimate of the costs, for which you start saving ahead of time.

PLAN AS EARLY AS POSSIBLE

Book as early as possible to keep travel costs down. Once you receive your "save the date", start putting plans in place as, especially if flights are involved, early birds tend to get the best prices. Even in the UK, the price of accommodation can potentially add hundreds to the total cost of attending a wedding or weekend party, so keep in mind that the most cost-effective option is unlikely to involve staying at the main venue. Instead of stretching your spending, browse a hotel booking platform or Airbnb to look for budget-friendly places to stay nearby to help keep your costs down.

SPLIT THE TRAVEL COSTS

With both hen parties and weddings, a significant chunk of the cost is typically associated with travel and accommodation, even more so when the destination is far from home or abroad. To keep costs down, look for ways to reduce your travel spending by car-sharing with other guests and booking trains or flights as early as possible. If you don't know the other hens attending, ask the organizers to connect you with someone whom you can share with. After all, you'll all get to know each other during the time away!

ATTEND WHAT YOU CAN

Don't be afraid to ask the event planners if you're struggling to fund the full itinerary. If attending the weekend-long celebration with all the bells and whistles breaks your budget, speak to the bridesmaids and discuss whether there's the possibility of joining for just a section of the day. Particularly if the event is spread across multiple days, explore going along for the daytime activities and skipping the evening. That can potentially save you the hefty cost of overnight accommodation (and probably a serious hangover too).

RE-WEAR AND RESELL YOUR OUTFIT

Say goodbye to the days of buying a new dress for every wedding you land an invitation to. Wearing the same outfit more than once is not only the best thing for your bank balance, but it's more sustainable as well. No one remembers what the guests wear at a wedding as all eyes are on the bride and groom, so don't feel any pressure to get a new outfit. If you do fancy a wedding wardrobe refresh, try reselling your outfits on a second-hand platform to fund your next investment piece.

SAYING I . . . DON'T

Even with the best will in the world, there's a chance that you'll find yourself in a situation where you have to decline an invitation to a wedding, hen or party weekend away. Saying no to an invitation – wedding or otherwise – is something that doesn't come naturally to everyone. Especially when it's a question of attending an event with people who matter to you, turning down an invitation can be a hard task.

Rather than taking the view that declining an invitation is always a negative experience, reframe your perspective and think of setting financial boundaries as the act of self-care that it can be for your overall wellbeing. As we've already seen, financial health is equally important as our physical and mental health, yet we often fail to give it the same care and attention. The pressure to attend events and spend more than you can allocate within your budget can really take its toll, so saying no can be essential to looking after your finances. Your friends will hopefully understand, having been there themselves at times. After all, life can be expensive and we all have our own resources and responsibilities.

To find out how to best navigate those sorts of situations, I asked Julia Boyd, founder of The Etiquette Consultant, for some tips on the best way to decline a wedding or party invitation without causing a rift with the hosts. First things first, should you give a reason for your response? She told me, "There is no obligation to give a reason to decline any invitation. I would suggest a polite apology for being unable to attend if you don't want to share your reason. For example, 'I'm so sorry I can't be there on that day. I can't wait to hear all about it later' should suffice." Tempting as it may be to come up with an excuse, Julia advises against this course of action. "It's better to give no reason than to lie. Fabricating a story or excuse is never a good idea. If the invitation is from someone close to you, it would be better to call them and try to give them an explanation for declining."

DECLINING AN INVITATION

If you find yourself in the tricky position of having to say no to an invite, take note of the following checklist from an etiquette expert:

- Whether or not you can attend an event, respond in a timely manner and if a date is specified for an RSVP then be sure to reply before the deadline.

- Any RSVP should be done in the same manner as the invitation was extended, whether you are declining or not. So if you received a formal written wedding invitation, the response should be written and formal.

- With close friends and family, along with the RSVP then a phone call will be appreciated if you're declining, even if it's just to say sorry you cannot attend.

- Remember you are under no obligation to explain your financial restrictions to anyone. However, it might be helpful to have an honest conversation with close family members or friends to avoid any bad feelings.

Whether you love a big party or you're happy at home with your pyjamas on, it's safe to say that celebrations can be brilliant, hilarious, stressful and eye-wateringly expensive in modern times. It's natural to want to celebrate milestones with your nearest and dearest, from the traditional weddings and birthdays, through to the equally worthy events like quitting a toxic job or leaving an unhealthy relationship. After all, special moments are where we so often make core memories that last. At the same time, the cost of celebrating can be endless, with diary dates booked months in advance and international trips galore, so keeping one eye on your bank balance during a busy social season is important to make sure you stay afloat financially. If you find yourself stressed or overstretched, don't be afraid to communicate with your friends about your situation and, if you need to, use the magic word: no. Looking after your financial wellbeing is essential to your wider wellbeing and no amount of partying – however much you'd like to head to Ibiza once again – is worth sacrificing that.

PREGNANT THEN SCREWED?

For many women, the idea of becoming a mother is one of the parts of adulthood they dream of from a young age. Even for those of us who don't aspire to have children or feel a maternal instinct, most of us will have been presented with baby dolls to care for and look after when we were only little girls ourselves. Whether you plan to become a parent or you're child-free by choice, traditional society has worked hard to instil the idea that a significant part of a girl's purpose on this planet is to care for and raise the next generation of children. Long before the realities of adulthood and the financial consequences of bringing up children come into play, society has told women since the dawn of time that their destiny is motherhood. Growing up, I didn't question the assumption that by my mid-20s, I'd be embarking on my own parenthood journey as my own mother had. The idea of having a child at 26 – my mother's age when I was born – didn't seem at all far-fetched or unrealistic when I was a child or teenager. Only when I entered the working world at 23 did it dawn on me that having children in my mid-20s was not going to happen, nor was it any longer the norm. During my 20s, it became clear that the age of first-time parents was on an upward trajectory.

Still, as soon as my 30th birthday was on the horizon, a noticeable shift in the social media content I consume started to take place. Less frequent were the posts where the majority of pictures from friends, acquaintances and influencers were exotic destinations and new outfits or handbags. Over a number of years, my social feeds shifted to become a constant announcement board for pregnancy scans, bump photos and gender reveals. No longer is there any element of surprise when yet another black-and-white scan photo appears and, at times, it can feel as though almost every person on the internet is having a baby. But the real picture couldn't be further from the truth, and outside of the social media bubble times are rapidly a-changing. The once-default path for women to settle down and become mothers at a certain point in time is being challenged – and for good reason, too.

Traditional expectations about what adulthood entailed used to look like a straightforward checklist: find a suitable partner, get married, buy a house and have 2.4 children. For many decades, deviating from the conventional path was unusual and whether people liked it or not, the path was rarely questioned. As the adage goes, if it ain't broke, don't fix it – and there were arguably few reasons to deviate from a trajectory which, in the sense that it provided stability and comfort for many, worked. Until eventually, it didn't. The conversation about motherhood has become increasingly complex, with more considerations for women to think about than ever before on the issue of whether or not to have children. From the impact of having children on your financial independence to the often eye-watering cost of childcare, never have there been more women and couples deciding to live a child-free life by choice. In a world where women have, in many respects, more options than ever before, are the financial implications of having a child fundamentally shifting the makeup of our society?

MAYBE, BABY

Over recent decades, the decision as to whether or not to have children has become more complicated for many adults, which has resulted in a long-term trend of falling fertility rates across countries such as the UK, the USA and China.[1] But why are more people on the fence about starting a family? Well, it seems that in the absence of the financial security and economic booms enjoyed by previous generations and amidst the backdrop of a climate crisis that our planet is enduring, more men and women are turning away from the well-trodden traditional path.

The decision about whether or not to have children is influenced by a whole host of factors, yet money is without a doubt becoming a more influential element – if not the most influential – in the outcome for many. For an increasing number of people who find themselves at a stage in their lives where they once imagined having children, the stark reality of the economic landscape – with its exorbitant housing costs, low wage growth and costly childcare systems – has made the prospect of bringing a new life, and an expensive one at that, into the world more challenging. In the US, the average cost of raising a child to the age of 18 now stands at over $300,000 ($17,000 per year).[2]

With increased political pressure in the UK following on from a huge amount of campaigning from groups such as Pregnant Then Screwed, much-needed change may be around the corner when it comes to childcare funding, but nothing is yet set in stone. Until significant policy changes that relieve the monumental pressure on working parents come into force, many would-be parents feel no choice but to set aside their desires and look at the decision to have a child or not as a purely financial one, however much they would like to bring a baby or two into the world.

Speaking to a cross section of women about their current feelings toward having children in the future, it's clear to see the conflicting feelings that many are trying to navigate. One woman, Rosie, is struggling with the urge to have a child and the knock-on consequences if she and her partner decide to do so. She tells me, "I already have that burning urge women describe [to have a child], but the amount of anxiety I have around it because of both financial situations and climate seems to be railroading me into depression." The clear-cut difference between the opportunities available to the previous generation compared to today only adds to her feelings of confusion about whether to have a child: "I sometimes get fed up with the lack of opportunities I feel like I have financially – especially when I compare my parents' lifestyle when they were my age, which I try not to do – and I think it'd be selfish to bring a child into this world." Whether you relate or not, it's clear to see that for many women what was once a straightforward decision is no longer so simple.

Fear of the ever-growing costs is what concerns Becky about having a child. Although she has always wanted kids, she worries that she will struggle to bring them up as she would like to do due to finances. She explains, "I think I'm leaning toward having them. All around I think the negatives don't matter as much because I want a family. But it's a difficult decision that I'm struggling very much to make."

Many women who do hope to have children one day are choosing to push back the point in time when they plan to start trying to get pregnant, so that they can focus on building financial security before children come into the picture. In 2020, for the first time since records started, half of the women aged 30 that year remained childless and the data suggests no sign of the trend changing direction any time soon.[3] When the news hit the headlines in a classic sensationalist manner, Twitter soon kicked into action and plenty of women weighed into the conversation, sharing their reasons why they didn't have children by the age of 30. Alongside the lack of a suitable partner, one reason why fewer 30-year-olds have children than ever before stood out loud and clear: the astronomical cost of raising children in the UK or USA and the impact of becoming a mother on career earnings. Many women in the discussion pointed to the fact that they had gone on to have children later in their 30s – however, only once they had a stable relationship and felt financially secure enough to deal with the inevitable costs of a child.

For others, the cost of raising children has influenced the number of children they decide to have, choosing to have only one child despite wanting more. The reality of raising a child in the current global economic climate is something that only hits home for many families once a baby arrives, regardless of the amount of preparation and planning ahead of time. Far from the baby boom years in the 1960s, when the average number of children that a woman had was 2.8, today the figure has fallen to 1.75, with no signs of an increase on the horizon.[4] The decline in the number of children per family isn't a UK-only phenomenon, either; by 2018 in the US, the average woman had approximately one biological child, compared to more than three in 1960.[5] Many families can feel a sense of guilt about being "one and done", partly as a result of the slew of negative connotations that attach to only children. Only children continue to be labelled with traits such as being spoilt and narcissistic, yet the root of these "traits" goes back to the Victorian era when the norm was very much to have several children, and only children were the outliers. Society peddled the narrative, continuing to push the idea that only children were doomed to be selfish and lacking in social skills, but it's unlikely to come as a surprise that studies in the 1980s completely debunked the stereotypes.[6] In fact, a study into the personality characteristics of only children found that in areas such as motivation and adjustment, only children scored better than other groups, but that on the whole only children and their sibling counterparts are highly comparable in most respects.[7] With no notable difference between only children and those with siblings, and in light of the hefty financial pressure families are facing, then it's easy to see why "one and done" is becoming more of a norm.

The impact on both her career and finances are the reasons why Claire decided to become a one-and-done parent, telling me, "I came under a lot of pressure to have more, including from my husband. It was interesting that my husband had absolutely zero concern for his career but I knew it would 100 per cent impact mine." Claire isn't alone in her decision, either. As she was the higher earner in the household, the financial strain that a second child would bring led Lou and her husband to settle on "one and done". She says, "We know we want to give our son a healthy life with lots of opportunities if possible. That means not working ourselves to death to provide for our child or leave them with nothing in terms of savings or assets, as we ourselves had to learn from our parents' mistakes."

Perhaps, then, it's time to ditch the outdated idea that having an only child is unfair on the child, or setting them up for a lonely life. With no sign of major systemic change on the horizon, the compelling reasons why many families are choosing to be "one and done" look likely to stay relevant, with the cost of childcare and the need for a bigger home high on the list. Rather than choosing to stretch themselves further financially, plenty of parents are content with focusing on raising one child with the love, attention and financial resources they have to give.

THE COST OF RAISING THE FUTURE

As unromantic as it might seem, having a child is increasingly becoming a financial investment in the world we live in. Much like any financial investment, whether a low-risk savings bank account or high-risk cryptocurrency, there are risks associated with the potential reward and, in a similar vein, many people take the plunge into the investment without fully knowing what they are signing up for. Regardless of whether we're talking about a child or company stock, knowledge gives you the best shot at making an informed decision. With that in mind, I asked a group of parents what they wished they knew before they had children. Here is what they told me:

> "I wish I had saved more and better paced my savings on maternity leave."

> "Should have looked into the cost of childcare."

> "It's at least twice as expensive as you think, so that money you're going to save – double it!"

> "In England, claim tax-free childcare. Lost two years' worth of help because no one told us about it."

> "Thirty hours of free childcare only covers 38 weeks in the year."

> "Companies will try and sell you overpriced gadgets that you don't need."

> "We felt pretty prepared for the financial hit, but the months without additional income were tough."

From the many parents I spoke to, it's plain to see that there are so many valuable nuggets of information they have to share, looking back. Experiences provide valuable lessons to learn from, and it certainly seems to be that one of the best things you can do financially is to prepare for the expected ahead of your baby's arrival, while knowing there will be things you cannot control once you have a small human to look after.

One of the key pieces of information that will help you plan financially is your maternity policy – both statutory and at work. All countries in the OECD have a national paid-leave policy for new mothers to ensure they are able to take time off work and continue to earn, for varying time periods, with one outlier: the United States. The US is the only country offering no national paid leave, requiring new mothers to rely solely on employer policies.[8] Under the law in England, Scotland and Wales, new mothers are entitled to statutory maternity pay (SMP) for up to 39 weeks at a rate of 90 per cent of your average weekly earnings before tax for the first six weeks, followed by £156.66 or 90 per cent of your average weekly earnings (whichever is lower) for the next 33 weeks.[9] Employers have the option to offer enhanced maternity pay, which can significantly impact your financial situation during maternity leave so if you are employed, do ask your workplace people team for the full details of the package available. Keep in mind that eligibility for enhanced maternity leave can kick in at different times, so you may need to work in a role for a specific period before you become fully eligible for the package.

For the self-employed and those without an enhanced maternity policy, the prospect of maternity leave can be daunting when it comes to money. In the UK, self-employed mothers can claim Maternity Allowance, which is paid at the same rate as SMP, yet this leaves many parents with a significant financial shortfall compared to their typical income. Planning ahead and starting to save as soon as having children is on the cards can give you the flexibility to top up your statutory payments throughout your maternity leave and allow a little more breathing room during those months. When deciding how much time to take off for maternity leave, there isn't a right or wrong decision and for all families – whatever your means – money will play a part in the choice.

There's one often overlooked financial knock-on that becoming a mother can have on women: the huge drop in pension contributions after having a child, which, at the time it happens, can seem minor but over the course of a working life, can amount to tens of thousands. The gender pensions or retirement gap is more than double the size of the gender pay gap, with the average female pensioner in the UK receiving over 40 per cent less income than men, and in the United States over 30 per cent less.[10] But why? One major contributor is the motherhood penalty.[11] The motherhood penalty is the term used to describe the changes that tend to take place in the working lives of women after having children. These changes can have a significant impact on the future finances of women, leading to widening gender pay and pension gaps among women of childbearing age. The penalty exists because mothers are more likely to work part-time than men in order to take on childcare responsibilities. Reducing working hours to part-time has a long-term impact on not only pay and progression but critically pensions contributions, as these are tightly linked to pay. For some working mothers, the motherhood penalty can even exclude them from receiving workplace pension contributions altogether; in the UK, the qualifying earnings amount for automatic enrolment into a workplace pension scheme is £10,000, yet many women working part-time find themselves below this threshold. Although, at the time of writing, you can opt into your workplace pension scheme and receive employer contributions if you earn between £6,240 and £10,000, enrolment isn't automatic, so take note: wherever possible, opt in to your workplace pension scheme or 401(k) and make the most of any employer contribution to top up your pension pot.[12] Future you will thank me later.

FUNDING FERTILITY

Dealing with the costs of having a baby and raising a child is a universal experience for those who find themselves pregnant, yet there's another major cost that can come with the desire to have children. From an early age, women of all ages will relate to the fear instilled by school and society alike around accidental pregnancies. Without pinpointing one specific influence or moment, as a teenager the issue of pregnancy and the narrative that it could ruin your life took hold, especially among the circles I found myself in. For a generation of schoolgirls, the prospect of accidentally falling pregnant kept them up at night and their only concern around fertility was avoiding pregnancy for as long as possible. From the media stories to the school sex education lessons, never would you think that in fact one in seven couples have difficulty conceiving.[13] Unsurprisingly, when you spend so many years of your life avoiding pregnancy, couples who find themselves struggling to fall pregnant can be shocked by the situation and, sometimes, the cost of the options in front of them.

Although support may be available in the UK on the NHS, only after at least one year of trying to fall pregnant can couples start to investigate; and in many cases, access to fertility treatment can take several years and eligibility often depends on the area you live in. For same-sex couples who hope to become parents, the majority of options involve fertility treatment which may or may not be available through the NHS. Additionally, for couples wishing to pursue the surrogacy route to parenthood, private treatment is required. In short, if you want to speed up the fertility process there's usually only one option: to pay. The cost of private treatment can be a huge financial hurdle for couples or individuals who dream of having children, yet it's one which isn't all that well publicized and, for many people, only when they realize they may struggle to conceive naturally does it become front of mind.

For Nicky and her husband, exploring private treatment came after a year of trying to conceive and not falling pregnant. She explains, "We were told it was 'unexplained infertility' and we'd therefore have to try for another year before we qualified for further assessment or intervention. We didn't want to wait that long so we started the process of fertility treatment then." Nicky and her husband eventually had two children with the help of IVF treatment, which didn't come at a small cost: "I knew it wouldn't be cheap, but I guess I didn't know the exact amounts. I think each round from scratch was about £10k all-in (ouch)." For couples with the financial means to fund private fertility treatment, having the children you dream of can become a reality in a relatively short space of time. But with long NHS waiting lists and a postcode lottery for fertility treatment across the UK, accessing fertility support without the ability to pay privately can be a long road.

THE COST OF THE BIOLOGICAL CLOCK

The female biological clock is a topic that, uncomfortable as it may be, is playing an increasingly notable role in the finances of many women. Partly driven by the pandemic and the realizations that many of us came to about our lives during that time, and in part driven by scientific progress in the process, egg freezing in the UK increased in popularity. In fact, even prior to the pandemic egg freezing procedures increased tenfold in the decade between 2009 and 2019.[14] While the primary reason given for freezing eggs is not having a partner, an NYU survey found that career concerns play a part, with 24 per cent of women reporting that they were freezing their eggs for professional reasons.[15] Financial stability is another factor influencing the decision to delay children; the cost of raising a child is another reason why 15 per cent of women in the NYU study chose to freeze their eggs in order to wait longer to have children and minimize the financial stress when the time comes.

For some women, egg freezing can provide a feeling of control and comfort if you're not yet ready to try to conceive. However, in 2023, the UK fertility regulator called for an urgent update to the laws around egg freezing over growing concerns that clinics aren't being fully transparent about the emotional, physical and financial costs of the process.[16] Not only that, but aggressive marketing tactics used by some clinics can make egg freezing seem like a sure-fire way to have a baby at a later date, rather than a chance that may not come to fruition. Due to the success rates, experts advise that it should be viewed as a way of increasing your chances of a successful pregnancy down the line and "a lottery ticket rather than having an insurance policy".[17] If you do decide to freeze your eggs, keep in mind that it isn't a cheap process, with (at the time of writing) the average cost of egg collection and freezing totalling £3,350 or anywhere from $4,500 to $8,000 in the US with medication on top costing several thousands more. And that's before you add in storage, thawing and transfer costs, bringing the total close to five figures.[18] So yes, you can pay for the potential to boost your odds of having a baby later in life, but like many things, it doesn't come for free.

In many respects, the future is bright for fertility options: there are more choices available to women than ever before, empowering us to make positive decisions about our futures. Yet still it's clear that there's a financial barrier in place; access to treatments and support is expensive, giving individuals with the funds to pay for fertility treatment a greater chance of becoming parents than those without. The considerable financial resources needed both to fund fertility treatment and to raise a child leaves me asking one question: is having a child now a privilege, rather than a universal option? Only time will tell.

WHAT TO EXPECT BEFORE YOU'RE EXPECTING

Although the well-known pregnancy guide *What to Expect when You're Expecting* talks about the many things you need to think about when you're actually pregnant, in an ideal world the financial planning will start before you're expecting a child. Before you fall pregnant, having a plan for how to manage the financial impact of welcoming a baby – from the maternity leave you take, through to the childcare years – can relieve a huge amount of stress and pressure at a time when you have plenty of other things to think about. Tempting as it may be to wait until you fall pregnant to start saving, there's no timeline set in stone for how quickly things might happen, so thinking ahead can put you in the best financial position to handle the inevitable costs of children. When you start to build your baby budget, there are a number of key questions to ask and one way to approach the finances is to break down the expected costs and change in income over the different stages of your maternity journey.

THE NEWBORN NUMBERS

For any new parent, the first year of having a child can be a shock to the system, both in terms of your everyday lifestyle and the financial changes. Even for families with the most generous maternity pay packages, which may cover up to six months' full pay, parents wishing to take a year off work to spend time with their new family member can find themselves with a substantial income shortfall every month for a sustained period. Work out the household take-home pay during each month of maternity or paternity leave, factoring in how long you each plan to take off work. Depending on parental leave options and your preferences as a family, you may wish to run the numbers for various scenarios to see what options you have financially. Once you have an idea about your income, turn your attention to expenses and have a look at whether you may be able to save money in any areas to free up more income for the new arrival.

Check your eligibility for any government or state support and make sure you claim any money you may be entitled to. In England, if you're expecting your first child and currently receive certain benefits, you might be able to get a Sure Start Maternity Grant, which is a one-off payment of £500 toward the costs associated with having a child.[19] Pregnant women also qualify for free dental care in the UK and free prescriptions in England during your pregnancy and for a year after you give birth. In the US, support available varies widely across states; however, low-income families may be eligible for financial assistance with bills, nutrition and housing.

There are inevitably going to be a fair few new items you need when you have a baby, especially for the first time. Essential items such as a cot, car seat, pram and bottles are absolute necessities and before long, the costs of must-haves can start to add up quickly. Where you can, speak to other parents in your network if possible to get a clearer idea of what you do actually need, as well as where you may be able to borrow items for a short period of time. Even if you don't have parent friends nearby, join a local prenatal group in your neighbourhood or download an app such as Peanut to connect with other mothers-to-be at a similar stage of their pregnancy journey to you.

It's natural to want to buy everything brand new for your baby, but there's a good chance you don't actually need every cute muslin or pair of booties you see. Yes, baby trainers may just be the cutest thing on the planet, but they probably aren't the best use of your cash. Focus on buying the basics new, and think outside the box when it comes to buying non-essential items. There are plenty of ways to save money on baby items and with second-hand resale platforms at our fingertips, finding perfect quality clothes for your newborn couldn't be quicker. Plus remember that babies grow very quickly and any teeny, tiny outfits you buy will likely only last a week or two, so shop for preloved options to help your budget stay healthy. Don't forget that as your little one grows out of each size of clothes, you can always resell them and send them to another home.

BABY ESSENTIALS CHECK-LIST

The essential items you need during the first year of parenthood include:

- crib or Moses basket

- buggy*

- play mat*

- high chair*

- cot, mattress, sleeping bags

- baby carrier or sling*

- car seat

- monitor*

- clothes*

- nappies* (if re-usable, obv!)

- muslins

- toys*

- books*

*indicates items you can purchase second-hand on a resale platform.

THE BACK-TO-WORK FINANCES

When your maternity leave ends, whether after a couple of months or after the maximum of 52 weeks in the UK if you choose to take the full entitlement, the next phase of costs involved with raising a child kick in: childcare fees. Although fewer than one in five new mothers returns to work full-time in the first three years after maternity leave, many women return to work part-time in order to balance childcare with earnings.[20] The reason for mothers working part-time rather than full-time isn't purely out of choice, either; one UK study found that despite 98 per cent of mums wanting to return to work after having children, only 13 per cent believed it to be viable on a full-time basis – predominantly because of the cost of childcare.[21]

According to the Organisation for Economic Co-operation and Development (OECD), the UK has one of the highest costs of childcare in the world, with parents on an average wage spending nearly a third of their income on nursery fees. In stark comparison, the equivalent couple in Germany spend just 1 per cent of their income on childcare due to the state-funded childcare system, which sharply contrasts with the exorbitant fees in the UK.[22] The financial impact of childcare on parents in Britain is such that a staggering three in four mothers surveyed by Pregnant Then Screwed stated that it no longer makes financial sense for them to work, with 11 per cent of parents saying that childcare costs are now the same or more than their daily take-home pay.[23]

It's clear to see that the UK childcare system is in crisis, with the spiralling costs making it increasingly difficult for families across various income levels to make ends meet, and unfortunately the situation mirrors that in the US, with the majority of households – particularly low-income and middle-class families – finding childcare unaffordable. In the UK, the typically higher salaries found in London are offset with the higher nursery fees, with the average full-time childcare place in 2022 for a child under two costing £269.86 per week across Great Britain, hitting a high of an average £368.73 per week for a nursery in London.[24] Add on top the cost-of-living crisis, along with childcare provider funding that fails to keep businesses afloat, and the full picture of the childcare sector crisis soon comes into focus. On average, US households are spending 27 per cent of their household income on childcare expenses and the rising costs don't appear to be slowing down.[25]

The cost of childcare means that for mothers, who are more likely to be the lower earners than fathers, the financial rationale for staying in work is becoming weaker. The result is that for certain women, the desire to further their career and maintain financial independence means that they can find themselves spending their entire salary on nursery fees each month in the hope that remaining in their career will pay off in the long term. The figures are crystal clear: invest in the childcare sector and the entire economy will benefit from more mothers in the workplace. Give women the choice to return to work and, for those who want it, the opportunity to build a career they love. The incentive for funding a childcare system properly is there for all, and at the time of writing, hope may be on the horizon. So while it remains to be seen what changes come into force over the coming years, the cries for financial support from parents finally seem to have been heard.

THE HIDDEN COSTS

Once your child hits three years old, the cost of childcare can start to decrease, although it certainly doesn't stop. In England, parents may be able to get up to 30 hours of funded childcare through the government (Scotland, Wales and Northern Ireland have different schemes), yet the hours are term-time only and stretched over 52 weeks. Parents also pay for extras such as meals and nappies on top, so while the hours help the costs come down, nursery still is by no means free.

For school-age children, wraparound care for working parents isn't always available, so either a nanny or childminder may be required at an additional cost, especially for parents who need to travel to and from work outside of school hours. And don't forget about those extra-curricular classes, holiday camps and birthday parties.

Whichever way you cut it, children can be extremely expensive and while you can't anticipate every cost in advance or control all of the expenditure, it's helpful to have an idea of what may lie ahead. Of course, there are plenty of families who raise happy children without endless extra costs involved because, after all, more than anything else children need security, attention and love.

TACKLING KEY CONVERSATIONS WHEN YOU'RE EXPECTING

When you find out you're expecting a child, plenty of things can race through your mind and one of the main thoughts can be the impact of your pregnancy on your work and career. There is no blueprint or universal approach to pregnancy and work; every woman will feel differently about their career, whether or not they plan to return to paid work in the future. For some, the juggle of work and motherhood may be low down the list of priorities, while for others, figuring out how best to manage your career and raise a child will be front of mind. If you find yourself in the latter camp, here's what you need to know about how to navigate some of the key conversations about your career in the near future.

DISCUSSING PROGRESSION AT WORK

Pregnancy and motherhood can add a new dimension to your career, especially if you currently enjoy your work and plan to continue your role in the same capacity when you return after having a child. Preparing yourself during pregnancy to navigate the journey of building a work life that you love alongside motherhood can set you up well to succeed, so be proactive about your career during your pregnancy and you can thrive through this new phase of your life. Tobi Asare, founder of My Bump Pay and author of *The Blend*, believes that pregnancy should not be a barrier to career moves or progression, having worked with many women to successfully secure promotions during pregnancy. She says, "I believe it's 100 per cent possible to perform at work while pregnant. The best piece of advice I can share is: make sure you have absolute clarity on what is expected of you in your role and what excellence looks like – and ruthlessly focus on those things. It's fine to focus on these things to ensure you are delivering to the best of your ability and, while you do so, don't forget to nurture and maintain relationships."

Keep your confidence high during your pregnancy by making note of your achievements at work, whether you're employed or work for yourself. Getting into the habit of keeping a record of your wins, successes and feedback – whether or not you're pregnant – is a brilliant way to make sure you're ready to put yourself forward for any opportunities that come your way, or to negotiate a pay rise in your next performance review. There's absolutely no reason why pregnancy should impact your ability to advocate for yourself, so back yourself with data.

EXPLORING PARENTAL LEAVE WITH A PARTNER

As the saying goes, it takes two to tango and in most cases, there are two parents actively involved in bringing a new child into the world. While there's a biological explanation for why women typically become the primary caregiver for the early days and weeks after childbirth, societal expectations have contributed to the fact that many women take the full load of childcare responsibilities during the first year of their child's life. Shared parental leave aimed to tackle the assumption that childcare is the mother's role, but the numbers of parents opting to make use of the policy are staggeringly low, with uptake in the UK as low as 2 per cent of eligible parents.[26] There are significant barriers, both practical and social, which contribute to the low uptake of shared parental leave; however, it's important to explore the conversation with your partner – especially if your preference is to split the first year of childcare between both of you.

If you plan to discuss the topic with your partner, lay the foundations by presenting the well-documented benefits of both parents or caregivers spending quality time with a baby early on. In a typical heterosexual family, discuss the many perks of father-and-baby bonding that come with spending time with a child at a very young age. The interactions between a father and their baby early on can influence their relationship over the long term, as the more time that a father spends getting to know their child, the more they understand the baby's signals and behaviour, so they can ultimately parent more effectively.[27] Further, studies looking at the effects of fathers taking parental leave have shown the impact to be overwhelmingly positive for the child and both parents, with 90 per cent of men who take leave noticing an improvement in their relationship with their partner.[28] Simply put, when fathers take leave the burden of responsibility is split more evenly between parents, rather than being heavily weighted on the mother.

ASKING FOR SUPPORT FROM GRANDPARENTS

Before diving into this discussion, it's important to acknowledge that everyone will have vastly different relationships with their parents. The options available to each family will vary hugely, based on a whole host of factors, and although all your friends may get free childcare from their parents, there isn't a single universal approach. Whether or not grandparents can help out with childcare often depends on their proximity to your home, their work status and finances, and their own capacity as well as their desire to be hands on. After all, many people in their 60s look forward to slowing down a little and taking on less work, not chasing around after a small child. So unless you've explicitly been told that help is on hand, it's better not to assume that your parents will be available for childcare help without having a candid conversation first with them.

If you plan to ask for help, rather than being vague then think about the specific request you have in mind before you start the conversation. For someone responding to a request for help, knowing exactly what the demands are will make it far easier for them to say yes or no. With family, being frank about the reasons for your request can help, too, whether it's purely financial, work related or otherwise. Finally, determine whether you plan to offer payment to a grandparent. While there's no right or wrong approach, if there's potentially expense involved in travelling to you, for example, an offer to cover costs may well be appreciated.

❧

The decision to become a parent is one of the biggest choices that many people will make, and it's by no means guaranteed that it will be a straightforward journey to parenthood either. The financial implications of the decision to have children, perhaps unforeseen fertility challenges and raising a child can be huge. But like many things in life, knowledge really is the key to empowering yourself to make better-informed financial decisions that align with your wider family goals. Whether you ultimately decide to be child-free, you're on the fence or you plan to go down the path of parenthood, the more control you have over your money, the more options you have to make parenthood work for you.

CONCLUSION

THE FUTURE OF YOUR FINANCIAL WELLBEING

As I'm someone who spends their every day talking about financial wellbeing, there are plenty of people who jump to the conclusion that I've found the answer, or nailed the formula for maintaining perfect financial wellbeing all the time. That couldn't be further from the truth. Like every other mere mortal, how I feel and behave with money shifts in line with the other events and goings-on in my life. That's not to say things don't change; once upon a time, my reaction to any strong positive or negative emotions involved spending to reward myself, whereas nowadays, I find myself overthinking purchases. As you may have gathered while reading this book, it's never straightforward with money.

Yet having explored so many formative moments through our lives where money and society intersect, hopefully by now you are at peace with the fact that our relationship with money isn't linear; rather, it's a squiggly, confusing journey of highs and lows. There will be times in your life where you prioritize your financial wellbeing, you feel calm and in control of your money and are confident about the future financially. That moment when you look at your savings account and feel a sense of achievement, or you negotiate that boost to your salary. There will also be times when you feel stressed and anxious, whether it's when your car unexpectedly fails a service and you get landed with an unexpected bill, or your landlord announces an 8 per cent rent rise without warning. All that is to say that financial wellbeing isn't an end in itself, and my hope is that this book serves as a companion and guide for those moments throughout life where you need a gentle reminder to give yourself a slice of financial self-care.

STEPS FOR FUTURE FINANCIAL WELLBEING

Before I sign off, here are a few final thoughts that I would like to share with you to encourage you on your journey to better lifelong financial wellbeing.

Give yourself grace

I'd love to tell you that once you've read this book, you'll have waved a magic wand to remove any future financial stresses or challenges from your life. The truth is that your journey with money will be a lifelong one and a work in progress. Give yourself grace for the dead ends you find yourself down, and the hurdles you hit. Nobody – not even the American billionaire Warren Buffett – has financial wellbeing totally nailed down.

Know your numbers

As much as your relationship with money influences your behaviour and decisions, starting to improve your financial wellbeing involves a practical element and knowing your numbers is essential to moving forward. Without a clear idea of where you are right now financially – knowing how much you have coming in and going out of your bank account each month – you're effectively trying to drive a car blindfolded. And we all know how that's likely to end . . .

Commit to learning

One of the best parts about learning in the 21st century is that teaching yourself a new skill or improving your knowledge on a topic no longer feels like you're stuck in a classroom, being forced to memorize algebra. There are so many brilliant books, podcasts, social channels and videos out there to help you to stay on track with your financial wellbeing. Turn to the resources guide at the back of this book for a head start.

Think money mindfulness

The more tuned in you become to where the money you spend truly enhances your life and where you find yourself impulse spending, the sooner you will begin to tune out the noise of marketing that encourages you to spend endlessly and, instead, find it easier to make more conscious spending decisions that align with your wider goals. It's not always easy, but spending mindfully really is rewarding and eliminates that feeling of buyer's regret.

Start talking about money

Talking about money with your friends, family and colleagues really is one of the most impactful things you can do to improve your financial health. The reluctance of society to open up about money holds us back in so many ways, yet the power is yours to change the narrative. From sharing experiences, supporting each other and shining a light on inequalities and injustices, being open about money has endless upsides.

Look after future you

In tough economic times, it can be challenging to think further ahead than the present. But time flies by quickly, and one of the greatest financial assets you have right now is time. For long-term wealth building, whether that's your retirement account or other investments, the sooner you start setting money aside then the longer it has to work for you. However much you can put away now, future you will thank you.

NOTES

INTRODUCTION

1 See: Suzanne McGee and Heidi Moore, "Women's Rights and Their Money: A Timeline from Cleopatra to Lilly Ledbetter", *Guardian*, 11 Aug 2014. Available at: www.theguardian.com/money/us-money-blog/2014/aug/11/women-rights-money-timeline-history (accessed 6 Jun 2023).

2 Hazel Ramsell, "The 2019 UK Financial Wellbeing Survey", Perkbox website, 25 Nov 2019. Available at: www.perkbox.com/uk/resources/blog/financial-wellbeing-survey (accessed 6 Jun 2023).

LIVE TO WORK, OR WORK TO LIVE?

1 Lucy Skoulding, "How Long Does The Average UK Employee Spend at Work?", AccountancyAge website, 2 Oct 2018. Available at: www.accountancyage.com/2018/10/02/how-long-does-the-average-uk-employee-spend-at-work/ (accessed 6 Jun 2023).

2 World Economic Forum (2020), Global Gender Gap Report 2020.

3 "Women in the Workplace 2020", Five Fifty, McKinsey Quarterly, n.d. Available at: www.mckinsey.com/featured-insights/diversity-and-inclusion/five-fifty-the-pandemics-gender-effect (accessed 6 Jun 2023).

4 Vicky Spratt, "Let 2020 Be The Year We Get Rid Of Girlboss Culture For Good", Refinery29 website, 20 Jan 2020. Available at: www.refinery29.com/en-gb/2020/01/9044921/girlboss-culture-women-work (accessed 7 Jun 2023).

5 Michael Grove, "Effects of Recession on the Graduate Labour Market", Prospects Luminate website, Feb 2018. Available at: luminate.prospects.ac.uk/effects-of-recession-on-the-graduate-labour-market (accessed 7 Jun 2023).

6 Catherine Rampbell, "Many with New College Degree Find the Job Market Humbling", *New York Times*, 18 May 2011.

7 "LSBF Careers Report Finds that 47% of UK Workforce Want a Career Change", London School of Business & Finance website, 18 Sep 2015. Available at: www.lsbf.org.uk/press-and-media/news-about-lsbf/2015/september-2015/lsbf-careers-report-finds-that-47-of-uk-workforce-want-a-career-change (accessed 19 Jun 2023).

8 "Salary and Benefits Review 2023", Tiger Recruitment website, 6 Mar 2023. Available at: tiger-recruitment.com/employers-and-hiring-practice/tiger-recruitment-salary-and-benefits-review/ (accessed 19 Jun 2023).

9 Emily T. Amanatullah and Michael W. Morris, "Negotiating Gender Roles: Gender Differences in Assertive Negotiating Are Mediated by Women's Fear of Backlash and Attenuated When Negotiating on Behalf of Others", *Journal of Personality and Social Psychology*, 98, no. 2 (2010): 256. Available at: gap.hks.harvard.edu/negotiating-gender-roles-gender-differences-assertive-negotiating-are-mediated-women%E2%80%99s-fear-backlash (accessed 19 Jun 2023).

FOR LOVE OR MONEY

1 Olivia Petter, "The Most Right-Swiped Jobs on Tinder Revealed", *Independent*, 5 Sept 2018. Available at: www.independent.co.uk/life-style/love-sex/tinder-most-right-swiped-jobs-nurse-interior-designer-pilot-dentist-a8523681.html (accessed 19 Jun 2023).

2 "2021 Couples & Money Study", Fidelity Investments website. Available at: www.fidelity.com/bin-public/060_www_fidelity_com/documents/about-fidelity/Fidelity-Couples-and-Money-Fact-Sheet-2021.pdf (accessed 19 Jun 2023).

3 Robert Booth, "Slump in Younger People Marrying Sparks Calls to Protect Cohabiting Rights", *Guardian*, 22 Feb 2021. Available at: www.theguardian.com/uk-news/2023/feb/22/slump-younger-people-marriage-protect-cohabiting-rights-england-wales (accessed 19 Jun 2023).

4 Wendy D. Manning and Lisa Carlton. "Trends in Cohabitation Prior to Marriage", *Family Profiles*, FP-21-04. Bowling Green, OH:

National Center for Family & Marriage Research, 2021. Available at: doi.org/10.25035/ncfmr/fp-21-04 (accessed 19 Jun 2023).

5 Lisa Roolant, "How People From Different Countries Feel About Discussing Salary", Insider website. Available at: www.businessinsider.com/discussing-salary-around-the-world-2014-3?r=US&IR=T (accessed 7 Jul 2023).

I'LL BE THERE FOR YOU

1 Fintan Smith, "State vs Private Education: How Much of a Difference Do Britons Think it Makes?" YouGov UK website, 16 Apr 2021. Available at: yougov.co.uk/topics/society/articles-reports/2021/04/16/state-vs-private-education-how-much-difference-do- (accessed 20 Jun 2023).

THE CURSE OF COMPARISON

1 Private correspondence.

2 CAP News, "Weight-Lss and Detoxing: Cut Out the Bad Stuff and Ensure a Balanced Diet of Responsibility and Evidence", Committees of Advertising Practice, 26 Jan 2023. Available at: www.asa.org.uk/news/weight-loss-and-detoxing-cut-out-the-bad-stuff-and-ensure-a-balanced-diet-of-responsibility-and-evidence.html (accessed 21 Jun 2023).

3 Bel Jacobs, "Seven Ways Fashion Has Changed in the 2010s", BBC website. Available at: www.bbc.com/culture/article/20191209-seven-ways-fashion-has-changed-in-the-2010s (accessed 21 Jun 2023).

4 See, for example, Harvard Medical School, "Giving Thanks Can Make You Happier", Harvard Health Publishing website, 14 Aug 2021. Available at: www.health.harvard.edu/healthbeat/giving-thanks-can-make-you-happier (accessed 21 Jun 2023).

THE BANK OF MUM AND DAD

1 Faiza Mohammad, Nina Mill and Kanak Ghosh, "Marriages in England and Wales: 2019", Office of National Statistics website, 19 May 2022. Available at: www.ons.gov.uk/peoplepopulationandcommunity/birthsdeathsandmarriages/marriagecohabitationandcivilpartnerships/bulletins/marriag

esinenglandandwalesprovisional/2019#first-marriages-and-remarriages (accessed 21 Jun 2023).

2 Ed Magnus, "Boomerang Generation: Almost One in Five Parents Expect Adult Children to Move Back into the Family Home Because of Rising Living Costs", 18 Feb 2023. Available at: www.thisismoney.co.uk/money/mortgageshome/article-1176 3167/Boomerang-generation-One-five-expect-adult-children-home.html (accessed 21 Jun 2023).

3 Rob Warnock, "2019 Millennial Homeownership Report", Apartment List website, 19 Nov 2019. Available at: www.apartmentlist.com/research/2019-millennial-homeownership-report (accessed 7 Jul 2023).

4 Sarah O'Conner, "Millennials Poorer than Previous Generations, Data Show", *Financial Times*, 23 Feb 2013. Available at; www.ft.com/content/81343d9e-187b-11e8-9e9c-25c814761640 (accessed 7 Jul 2023).

5 Marcus Lu, "Is the American Dream Over? Here's What the Data Says", World Economic Forum website, 2 Sep 2023. Available at: www.weforum.org/agenda/2020/09/social-mobility-upwards-decline-usa-us-america-economics/ (accessed 21 Jun 2023).

6 "From Student Grants to Tuition Fees", *Guardian*, 23 Jan 2003. Available at: www.theguardian.com/politics/2003/jan/23/uk.education (accessed 21 Jun 2023).

7 Susan Hubble and Paul Bolton, "Higher Education Tuition Fees in England", House of Commons Library website, 25 Jun 2018. Available at: commonslibrary.parliament.uk/research-briefings/cbp-8151/ (accessed 21 Jun 2023).

8 Melanie Hanson, "Average Cost of College & Tuition", Education Data Initiative website, 25 Jun 2023. Available at: educationdata.org/average-cost-of-college/ (accessed 7 Jul 2023).

9 Laura Brown, "Student Money Survey 2022 – Results", Save the Student website, 20 Sep 2022. Available at: www.savethestudent.org/money/surveys/student-money-survey-2022-results.html (accessed 21 Jun 2023).

10 Bill Davies et al, "Lessons from Germany: Tenant Power in the Rental Market", IPPR website, 16 Jan 2017. Available at: www.ippr.org/publications/lessons-from-germany-tenant-power-

in-the-rental-market#:~:text=German%20tenants%20enjoy%20 strong%20security,initial%20contract%20period%20without%20 justification. (accessed 21 Jun 2023).

11 Nigel Wilson, "U.S. Millennials: Home Ownership and the Growing Chasm Between Aspiration and Reality", Forbes website, 18 Aug 2012. Available at: www.forbes. com/sites/nigelwilson/2021/08/18/us-millennials-home-ownership-and-the-growing-chasm-between-aspiration-and-reality/?sh=5d453de25498 (accessed 7 Jul 2023).

12 Duncan Lamont, "What 175 Years of Data Tell Us About House Price Affordability in the UK", Schroders website. Available at: www.schroders.com/en/insights/economics/what-174-years-of-data-tell-us-about-house-price-affordability-in-the-uk/ (accessed 21 Jun 2023).

13 Michelle Delgado, "U.S. House Prices Are Rising Exponentially Faster Than Income (2021 Data)", Real Estate Witch website, 26 Jan 2023. Available at: www.realestatewitch.com/house-price-to-income-ratio-2021/ (accessed 7 Jul 2023).

14 Mortgage Advice Bureau, "The Bank of Mum and Dad is 9th Biggest Lender", Mortgage Advice Bureau website, n.d. Available at: www.mortgageadvicebureau.com/expert-advice/ first-time-buyer/the-bank-of-mum-and-dad-is-9th-biggest-lender (accessed 22 Jun 2023).

15 Bee Boileau and David Sturrock, "Bank of Mum and Dad Drives Increasing Economic Inequalities in Early Adulthood", IFS website, 13 Feb 2023. Available at: ifs.org.uk/news/bank-mum-and-dad-drives-increasing-economic-inequalities-early-adulthood (accessed 22 Jun 2023).

16 Ibid.

17 Money and Pensions Service, "Lifetime ISAs", MoneyHelper website, n.d. Available at: /www.moneyhelper.org.uk/en/ savings/types-of-savings/a-guide-to-lifetime-isas (accessed 22 June 2023).

18 HM Government, "The Mortgage Guarantee Scheme", Own Your Own Home website, n.d. Available at: www. ownyourhome.gov.uk/scheme/mortgage-guarantee-scheme/ (accessed 22 Jun 2023).

19 Dan Green, "14 First-Time Home Buyer Grants and Programs in 2023", homebuyer.com website, 19 may 2023. Available at: homebuyer.com/learn/first-time-home-buyer-grants-programs (accessed 7 Jul 2023).

YOU'RE INVITED

1 Nick Stripe, "Married by 30? You're Now in the Minority", Office for National Statistics website, 1 Apr 2019. Available at: blog.ons.gov.uk/2019/04/01/married-by-30-youre-now-in-the-minority/ (accessed 22 Jun 2023).

2 Rebecca Lake, "What is the Average Age of Marriage in the U.S.?", *Bride* magazine website, 22 Ap 2022. Available at: www.brides.com/what-is-the-average-age-of-marriage-in-the-u-s-4685727 (accessed 7 Jul 2023).

3 Claire Flynn, "First-time Buyer Statistics and Facts: 2023", Money website, 6 Mar 2023. Available at: www.money.co.uk/mortgages/first-time-buyer-mortgages/statistics (accessed 22 Jun 2023).

4 GoHen blog, "Hen Party Statistics – 2022–2023 Industry Report", GoHen.com, 9 Mar 2023. Available at: www.gohen.com/blog/hen-party-statistics-2022-2023-industry-report/ (accessed 22 Jun 2023).

5 "Destination Wedding Statistics 2023", Condor Ferries website, n.d. Available at: www.condorferries.co.uk/destination-wedding-statistics#:~:text=There%20are%20350%2C000%20destination%20weddings,choose%20to%20get%20married%20overseas. (accessed 7 Jul 2023).

6 Zoe Burke, "How Much Does a Wedding Cost? The UK Average Revealed", *Hitched* website, 24 Jan 2023. Available at: www.hitched.co.uk/wedding-planning/organising-and-planning/the-average-wedding-cost-in-the-uk-revealed (accessed 19 Jun 2023).

PREGNANT THEN SCREWED?

1 The Week Staff, "What Declining Birth Rates Mean for Our Future", *The Week* website, 3 Oct 2022. Available at: www.theweek.co.uk/news/society/958081/what-declining-birth-rates-mean-for-our-future (accessed 22 Jun 2023).

2 Ahaba Bhattarai et al.,"What Does it Cost to Raise a Child?", *Washington Post* website, 13 Oct 2022. Available at: www. washingtonpost.com/business/interactive/2022/cost-raising-child-calculator/ (accessed 7 Jul 2023).

3 Amanda Sharfman, "Childbearing for Women Born in Different Years, England and Wales: 2020", Office for National Statistics website, 27 Jan 2022. Available at: www. ons.gov.uk/peoplepopulationandcommunity/birthsdeaths andmarriages/conceptionandfertilityrates/bulletins/child bearingforwomenbornindifferentyearsengland andwales/2020 (accessed 22 Jun 2023).

4 Aaron O'Neill, "Total Fertility Rate in the United Kingdom from 1800 to 2020*", Statista website, 21 Jun 2022. Available at: www.statista.com/statistics/1033074/fertility-rate-uk-1800-2020/ #:~:text=In%20the%20United%20Kingdom%20in,dropping%20 to%204.9%20by%201835. (accessed 22 Jun 2023).

5 Aria Bendix and Joe Murphy, "The Modern Family Size Is Changing: Four Charts Show How", NCB News website, 12 Jan 2023. Available at:www.nbcnews.com/health/parenting/ how-modern-us-family-size-changing-charts-map-rcna65421 (accessed 7 Jul 2023).

6 Genevieve Walker, "Why Only Children Are Still Stereotyped as Selfish and Spoilt", BBC website, 16 Nov 2021. Available at: www.bbc.com/worklife/article/20211116-why-only-children-are-still-stereotyped-as-selfish-and-spoilt (accessed 22 Jun 2023).

7 Denise F. Polit and Toni Falbo. "Only Children and Personality Development: A Quantitative Review", *Journal of Marriage and Family*, vol. 49, no. 2, 1987, pp. 309–25. JSTOR website, doi. org/10.2307/352302. (accessed 22 June 2023).

8 Miranda Bryant, "Maternity Leave: US Policy Is Worst on List of the World's Richest Countries", *Guardian*, 27 Jan 2023. Available at: www.theguardian.com/us-news/2020/jan/27/maternity-leave-us-policy-worst-worlds-richest-countries (accessed 7 Jul 2023).

9 Money and Pensions Service, "Maternity Leave and Pay", Money Helper website, n.d. Available at: www.moneyhelper. org.uk/en/family-and-care/becoming-a-parent/maternity-pay-and-leave (accessed 22 Jun 2023).

10 OECD, "Towards Improved Retirement Savings Outcomes for Women", OECD Publishing, Paris, 2021. Available at: www.oecd-ilibrary.org/sites/1b05af8e-en/index.html?itemId=/content/component/1b05af8e-en (accessed 7 Jul 2023).

11 Jude Gardner, "The Gender Pensions Gap: Tackling Motherhood Penalty", People's Partnership website, n.d. Available at: peoplespartnership.co.uk/media-centre/policy-research/the-gender-pensions-gap-tackling-the-motherhood-penalty/#:~:text=Our%20new%20report%2C%20'The%20gender,more%20if%20childcare%20was%20cheaper. (accessed 22 Jun 2023).

12 Laura Halloran, "Pensions: The Motherhood Penalty", Just Finance Foundation website. Available at: www.justfinance foundation.org.uk/news/pensionsandmotherhood (accessed 22 Jun 2023).

13 NHS, "Overview: Infertility", NHS website, n.d. Available at: www.nhs.uk/conditions/infertility/#:~:text=Around%201%20in%207%20couples,every%202%20or%203%20days). (accessed 22 Jun 2023).

14 Hannah Devlin, "'A Lottery Ticket, Not a Guarantee': fertility experts on the rise of egg freezing", Guardian, 11 Nov 2022. Available at: www.theguardian.com/society/2022/nov/11/not-a-guarantee-why-freezing-your-eggs-shouldnt-be-an-insurance-policy#:~:text=Egg%20freezing%20in%20the%20UK,almost%202%2C400%20cycles%20in%202019. (accessed 22 Jun 2023).

15 "Why Do Women Freeze Their Eggs?", Extend Fertility website, 1 May 2017. Available at: extendfertility.com/why-do-women-freeze-their-eggs/ (accessed 22 Jun 2023).

16 Miranda Bryant, "Warning for UK women over Physical and Financial Toll of Egg Freezing", Guardian, 8 Jan 2023. Available at: www.theguardian.com/society/2023/jan/08/warning-for-uk-women-over-physical-and-financial-toll-of-egg-freezing

17 Devlin, 2022.

18 Human Fertilisation and Embryology Authority, "Egg Freezing", HFEA website, n.d. Available at: www.hfea.gov.uk/treatments/fertility-preservation/egg-freezing/ (accessed 22 Jun 2023).

19 GOV.UK, "Sure Start Maternity Grant", GOV.UK website, n.d. Available at: www.gov.uk/sure-start-maternity-grant (accessed 23 Jun 2023).

20 "How Women's Employment Changes After Having a Child", Understanding Society website, 22 Oct 2019. Available at: www.understandingsociety.ac.uk/2019/10/22/how-womens-employment-changes-after-having-a-child (accessed 22 Jun 2023).

21 "Careers After Babies Report Highlights Alarming Statistics for Women Returning to Work After Having Children", WeAretheCity website, 3 March 2023. Available at: wearethecity.com/careers-after-babies-report-highlights-alarming-statistics-for-women-returning-to-work-after-having-children/ (accessed 23 Jun 2023).

22 Molly Blackall, "Childcare Costs: UK Parents Spend a Third of Income Compared to 1% in Germany, inews website, 15 Mar 2023. Available at: inews.co.uk/news/childcare-costs-uk-parents-income-daycare-fees-germany-2209649 (accessed 23 Jun 2023).

23 "New Pregnant Then Screwed Data Shows Three-Quarters of Mothers Who Pay for Childcare Say it Does Not Make Financial Sense for Them to Work", Pregnant Then Screwed website, n.d. Available at: pregnantthenscrewed.com/three-quarters-of-mothers-who-pay-for-childcare-say-that-it-does-not-make-financial-sense-for-them-to-work/ (accessed 23 Jun 2023).

24 Lester Coleman, Sam Shorto and Dalia Ben-Galim, "Childcare Survey 2022", n.d. Available at: www.familyandchildcaretrust.org/sites/default/files/Resource%20Library/Final%20Version%20Coram%20Childcare%20Survey%202022_0.pdf (accessed 23 Jun 2023).

25 Care.com Editorial Staff, "This is How Much Child Care Costs in 2023", Care.com website. 13 Jun 2023. Available at: www.care.com/c/how-much-does-child-care-cost/ (accessed 7 Jul 2023).

26 Matt Creagh, "Shared Parental Leave Isn't Working: New Parents Need Stronger Rights", TUC website, 5 Apr 2019. Available at: www.tuc.org.uk/blogs/shared-parental-leave-isnt-working-new-parents-need-stronger-rights (accessed 23 Jun 2023).

27 Maryam Abdullah, "How Paternity Leave Helps Dads and Babies Bond", *Great Good* Magazine website, 15 Jun 2022. Available at: greatergood.berkeley.edu/article/item/how_paternity_leave_helps_dads_and_babies_bond (accessed 23 Jun 2023).

28 Francesca Colantuoni, et al., "A Fresh Look at Paternity Leave: Why the Benefits Extend Beyond the Personal", McKinsey & Company website, 5 Mar 2021. Available at: www.mckinsey.com/capabilities/people-and-organizational-performance/our-insights/a-fresh-look-at-paternity-leave-why-the-benefits-extend-beyond-the-personal (accessed 23 Jun 2023).

FURTHER RESOURCES

Here you'll find a short guide signposting some of the leading resources to help you dive deeper into the topics covered throughout *Money Talks*, from websites to podcasts and beyond.

FOR A MONEY MINDSET

Clare Seal, *Five Steps to Financial Wellbeing* (Headline, 2022)
    A toolkit to help readers establish a positive relationship with money, Clare Seal walks through five achievable steps to take to change your relationship with money for the better.

Alex Holder, *Open Up: Why Talking About Money Will Change Your Life* (Serpent's Tail, 2019)
    Exploring the ways that opening up about money in all areas of your life can have a significant positive effect, Alex Holder provides insights and practical tips to encourage readers to talk about money more openly.

Morgan Housel, *The Psychology of Money* (Harriman House, 2020)
    Author Morgan Housel explores the way people think about money and breaks down the idea that doing well with money is about what you know or how smart you are.

FOR CAREER AND WORK

Career Happiness Podcast: www.somaghosh.com/podcast
    Careers adviser Soma Ghosh hosts the Career Happiness Podcast, offering careers advice to professional women and

business owners to help them grow their career, align it with their values and find career happiness.

Glass Door: www.glassdoor.co.uk/index.htm
Search for jobs, salary information, company reviews and interview questions.

The Guardian Careers: jobs.theguardian.com/careers
Extensive articles covering different aspects of career advice such as tips to address gaps on your CV, why you should never lie on your CV and industry-specific CV-writing tips.

LinkedIn: www.linkedin.com/business/sales/blog/profile-best-practices/17-steps-to-a-better-linkedin-profile-in-2017
Practical advice to create a better LinkedIn profile to increase your visibility and opportunities.

FOR RELATIONSHIPS

Combining Finances: www.unbiased.co.uk/discover/personal-finance/family/combined-finances-couples
Explanation of both the advantages and disadvantages of combining your finances as a couple.

Financial Support when You Separate: www.citizensadvice.org.uk/family/sorting-out-money/financial-support-when-you-separate/
How separating from a partner can have a big impact on your finances.

Living Together versus Married: UK Legal Differences: www.citizensadvice.org.uk/family/living-together-marriage-and-civil-partnership/living-together-and-marriage-legal-differences/
A breakdown of how different areas of finances are impacted depending on whether you are living together as a couple or are married.

Talking to Your Partner about Money: www.moneyhelper.
org.uk/en/family-and-care/talk-money/talking-to-your-partner-
about-money

Guides to various financial topics and how to discuss them with your partner.

FOR FAMILY FINANCES

ChildCare.gov: childcare.gov/

Comprehensive directory of free tools and resources organized by US states, including childcare financial assistance programs.

FreeWill: www.freewill.com

Free will-writing service available for those living in the United States.

Help with Childcare Costs: www.moneyhelper.org.uk/en/family-and-care/becoming-a-parent/help-with-childcare-costs

Detailed FAQ on help available within the UK for childcare, including eligibility criteria and how to apply for support and benefits.

Maternity Action: maternityaction.org.uk/advice/money-for-parents-and-babies/

An information sheet for pregnant people or parents of a newborn detailing what you may be able to claim and how to do it.

Pregnant Then Screwed: pregnantthenscrewed.com/

A charity dedicated to ending the motherhood penalty, supporting tens of thousands of women each year, and successfully campaigning for change.

Make A Will Online: farewill.com/make-a-will-online
Low-cost, simple-to-use will-writing service for UK citizens including approval by specialists.

FOR MONEY MANAGEMENT

Budget Planner: www.moneyhelper.org.uk/en/everyday-money/budgeting/budget-planner
Create and save your own budget to help you to know exactly where your money is being spent, and how much you've got coming in.

The Guide to Maximizing Your Money: www.nerdwallet.com/article/finance/personal-finance
Detailed online guide to the fundamentals of personal finance including making money, saving money, building wealth and protecting assets.

Laura Whateley, *Money: A User's Guide* (Fourth Estate, 2018)
A clear, practical handbook walking readers through all the basics you need to know about managing your money to make better informed financial decisions

Money Saving Expert: www.moneysavingexpert.com
A journalistic website providing money-saving guides, tips, tools and techniques. Also publishes a weekly email with deals and need-to-know financial updates.

FOR BUILDING WEALTH

Financial Feminist podcast: herfirst100k.com/financial-feminist-podcast
Focused on helping you feel financially confident, founder of Her First $100K shares resources and interviews to help listeners to save and grow their money.

Simran Kaur, *Girls That Invest: Your Guide to Financial Independence through Shares and Stocks* (Wiley, 2022)

A step-by-step guide to financial independence, breaking down all the jargon that surrounds investing in stocks and teaching the key principles that apply to investing across the globe.

Alice Ross, *Investing To Save The Planet: How Your Money Can Make a Difference* (Penguin Business, 2020)

Focused on a call to action for all investors, journalist Alice Ross reveals how green investing is an underutilized way to make a difference to the climate crisis without having to compromise on financial returns.

The Pension Confident podcast: www.pensionbee.com/podcast

Pensions can be complicated, so the PensionBee team is on a mission to simplify pensions for everyone. From the basics of personal finance to the bigger questions of pension planning, this podcast covers all the bases.

FOR HELP AND SUPPORT

Benefits Checker: www.gov.uk/check-benefits-financial-support

Find out if you are entitled to claim any UK benefits.

Citizens Advice: www.citizensadvice.org.uk/debt-and-money/

A UK charity and network of local charities offering confidential advice online, over the phone and in person for free.

Debt Help Organization: www.debt.org/

Supplying key information about debt management options with articles, tools and resources for US citizens.

Government Financial Help: www.nerdwallet.com/article/
finance/6-ways-to-get-free-money-from-the-government
 A summary of US federal and state grants and loans available for those struggling financially.

National Debtline: nationaldebtline.org/
 Speak to an expert debt adviser for free.

Stepchange: www.stepchange.org/
 Free, impartial and confidential debt advice and plans to help you pay off debt.

Turn2Us: www.turn2us.org.uk/
 A UK charity providing practical help to people who are struggling financially.

ACKNOWLEDGEMENTS

Writing this book is a dream come true and wouldn't have been possible without a huge team of supporters and contributors. Thank you to my editor, Lucy, for believing in the idea I had for a book about money that didn't fit the typical mould out there, and for endless understanding and support during the writing and editing process. To my agent, Oscar, for dropping into my inbox to ask whether I'd ever thought of writing a book only a few weeks after I scribbled "write my first book" on my vision board.

To all the brilliant contributors who have made the book what it is, from the TGTM community members who shared their personal stories and experiences so generously, to the roster of professional experts who have contributed their decades of experience. I am so grateful for the time and energy put into turning this book from an idea into a reality.

To all my family and friends, the ultimate cheerleaders behind the scenes who have ridden the emotional rollercoaster of building a business and writing a book alongside me. V, for being the person I trusted with the first words early on and for all your encouragement and feedback – I am eternally grateful.

To C (+ K), my little family bubble. I truly couldn't have done this without you. You believe in me more than I could ever imagine, and I am the luckiest person in the world to have you on my team.

And finally, thank you to every single person who has been part of the This Girl Talks Money community from day one or whether you've discovered us today. This book is for you.

ABOUT THE AUTHOR

Bored of the same old financial tips written by middle-aged white men in suits, Ellie started the online platform This Girl Talks Money to open up the conversation around earning, spending, saving and managing money. With a community of over 30K people, Ellie provides knowledge, insights and a safe space to help people gain confidence and ownership of their finances. Alongside building a community of financially empowered women, Ellie has worked with brands from eBay to *Glamour* to American Express, as well as providing financial expertise for Refinery29, *Stylist*, BBC News and more. Ellie is also the co-host of the podcast Money Unfiltered.

WATKINS
1893

The story of Watkins began in 1893, when scholar of esotericism John Watkins founded our bookshop, inspired by the lament of his friend and teacher Madame Blavatsky that there was nowhere in London to buy books on mysticism, occultism or metaphysics. That moment marked the birth of Watkins, soon to become the publisher of many of the leading lights of spiritual literature, including Carl Jung, Rudolf Steiner, Alice Bailey and Chögyam Trungpa.

Today, the passion at Watkins Publishing for vigorous questioning is still resolute. Our stimulating and groundbreaking list ranges from ancient traditions and complementary medicine to the latest ideas about personal development, holistic wellbeing and consciousness exploration. We remain at the cutting edge, committed to publishing books that change lives.

DISCOVER MORE AT:

www.watkinspublishing.com

| Read our blog | Watch and listen to our authors in action | Sign up to our mailing list |

We celebrate conscious, passionate, wise and happy living.

Be part of that community by visiting

 /watkinspublishing   @watkinswisdom
/watkinsbooks   @watkinswisdom